THE USPC GUIDE TO

LONGEING

AND

GROUND TRAINING

ALSO BY SUSAN E. HARRIS

THE USPC GUIDE TO
LONGEING
AND
GROUND TRAINING

written and illustrated by

SUSAN E. HARRIS

RUTH RING HARVIE, USPC EDITOR

Howell Book House
New York

This book is not intended as a substitute for professional advice and guidance. A
person should take part in the activities discussed in this book only under the
supervision of a knowledgeable adult.

Howell Book House
A Simon & Schuster Macmillan Company
1633 Broadway
New York, NY 10019

MACMILLAN is a registered trademark of Macmillan, Inc.

Library of Congress Cataloging-in-Publication Data

Harris, Susan E.
    The USPC guide to longeing and ground training / written and illustrated by Susan E.
Harris : Ruth Ring Harvie, USPC editor.
    p.   cm.
    ISBN 0-86705-640-0
    1. Longeing (Horsemanship)   I. Harvie, Ruth Ring.   II. United States Pony Clubs.
III. Title.
SF287.H36   1997
797.2'3—dc21   97-9403
                                                                              CIP

Manufactured in the United States of America

10 9 8 7 6 5 4 3 2

CONTENTS

ABOUT THE UNITED STATES PONY CLUBS, INC.

The United States Pony Clubs, Inc. is an educational youth organization that teaches riding, mounted sports, and the care of horses and ponies, and develops in youth the characteristics of responsibility, sportsmanship, moral judgment, leadership, and self-confidence.

Since its beginning in Great Britain in 1928, Pony Club has become the largest junior equestrian group in the world, with more than 125,000 members in 27 countries. At this writing, the U.S. Pony Clubs have approximately 11,000 members in more than 500 clubs. Members ride mounts of all breeds and sizes, not just ponies; the term "pony" originally referred to any mount ridden by a young person.

The U.S. Pony Clubs teach a curriculum which covers balanced seat horsemanship on the flat, over fences, and in the open, along with safety, knowledge and practical skills in horse care and management. The goal is to produce safe, happy, and confident horsepersons who can ride, handle, and care for their horse and equipment competently at their level, with an understanding of the reasons for what they do.

Pony Clubbers progress at their own pace through a series of levels or ratings, from D (basic) through C (intermediate) to B, HA, and A (advanced). The requirements for each rating are called the USPC Standards of Proficiency. The lower level ratings (D-1 through C-2) are tested within the local Pony Club; the C-3 rating is tested at a Regional Testing; and the B, HA, and A levels are national ratings, requiring advanced levels of knowledge, horsemanship, and horse care and management skills.

Besides instruction and ratings, Pony Club offers activities such as combined Training, Foxhunting, Dressage, Mounted Games, Show Jumping, Tetrathlon, and Vaulting, with emphasis on safety, teamwork, and good horsemanship and sportsmanship.

For more information about the U.S. Pony Clubs, please contact:

United States Pony Clubs, Inc.
The Kentucky Horse Park
Iron Works Pike
Lexington, KY 40511
(606) 254-PONY (7669)

INTRODUCTION

This book covers basic horse handling, ground training, and methods of longeing the horse and rider. The information contained here is drawn from the United States Pony Club Manuals of Horsemanship (Books One, Two, and Three, covering the USPC D through A Levels) and the USPC Standards of Proficiency. It is written for Pony Clubbers, instructors, and other horsepersons, adults, and young people who want to learn to longe, handle, and improve their horses' ground manners safely.

Proper handling, ground training, and longeing are fundamental to safety, effective training, and good horsemanship. Handling is the interface between horse and human; it establishes the relationship between the horse and his trainer. It often has been said that whenever you handle a horse, you are either training him, preserving his training, or spoiling his training, whether you are aware of it or not. The way you handle a horse from the ground, in leading and everyday chores as well as in longeing, influences the way he responds to riding and training under saddle.

When handling horses, safety must always come first, to prevent accidents to you, your horse, or other people. In this book you will find safety procedures for leading, handling, training, and longeing horses; *make it a rule to follow them every time you handle a horse*, whether you are training a young horse, working with a problem horse, or simply performing routine tasks, such as grooming, saddling, or bringing in horses from pasture.

Longeing is a common and convenient method of exercise and training the horse and rider, yet it is too often practiced in a sloppy, incorrect, or even dangerous manner. Because of the potential for injury to the horse, handler, and rider, longeing must be done properly, in a way that is safe and appropriate, by a competent, experienced handler. This is especially important when longeing a rider, because the rider's safety depends on your skill, competence, and judgment. It's essential to learn (and to teach your horse) the basic steps first, starting with proper leading and handling, ground manners, and voice commands, *before* trying to train a horse on the longe line.

This book explains the equipment, essentials, and safe, step-by-step methods for ground training, learning to longe a trained horse, longeing for various purposes, training the horse on the longe line, and longeing the rider. You will learn where and how long to longe, how to adjust and use longeing equipment, basic control techniques for longeing at all gaits, and how to improve and refine your control on the longe line. Longeing for warmup, exercise, and to improve the horse's movement and acceptance of the bit are covered, along with methods for teaching a horse to longe and for handling common longeing problems.

The U.S. Pony Clubs emphasize proper preparation and safe, logical, progressive methods. However, longeing, handling, and ground training are practical skills which cannot be acquired by reading a book. You will need hands-on instruction from a qualified person, and must work within the limits of your knowledge and experience while you are learning. Pony Clubbers learn about longeing at the C Level (intermediate), but should only longe trained horses, under supervision, until they reach an advanced level; this is a good policy for others as well.

Through correct, safe, and progressive ground work and longeing, working patiently and consistently, with awareness of how the horse moves and responds, you can improve your horse's training, movement and muscular development, while developing respect, communication, and trust between you and your horse.

THE USPC GUIDE TO

LONGEING

AND

GROUND TRAINING

CHAPTER 1

BASIC TRAINING PRINCIPLES

Horses have developed into the kind of creatures they are over more than 50 million years. The horse's natural instincts and characteristics, as well as each horse's individual nature and past experiences, affect the way he responds to training and to new situations.

THE HORSE'S NATURE AND BEHAVIOR

Because horses are prey animals, they depend on their keen senses to detect and flee from predators. This makes them easily frightened; a horse's first instinct is to run from danger. If a horse is frightened and can't escape, he may defend himself by kicking, striking, or running over anything in his way.

A horse's eyes are placed on the sides of his head so he can see all around him. However, he has two blind spots—behind his rump and right in front of his nose. If you come up on him in his blind spots without warning, he may be startled and might try to get away or kick before he knows who you are.

Horses have social behaviors that govern the way they act with other horses. Horses are herd animals by nature; they prefer to be with other horses. Domestic horses sometimes become attached to their stable as if it were their herd. Every herd has a "pecking order"; each horse has his own place, from the herd leader to the lowest ranking horse. Higher ranking horses use body language (sometimes biting or other aggressive behavior) to keep the lower ranking horses in their place. Horses react to the behavior of other horses; if one horse shies or takes off running, the others follow suit.

The horse's range of vision.

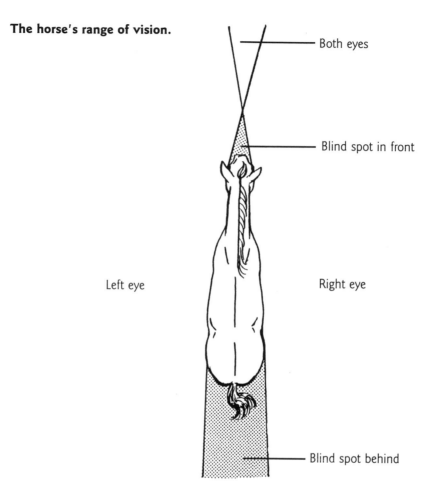

Both eyes

Blind spot in front

Left eye

Right eye

Blind spot behind

To train and handle a horse safely and successfully, you must understand his nature and behavior, and you must have his attention, respect, and trust. Your horse should regard you as a trustworthy herd leader, not as a threat or a lower ranking horse. A good trainer projects an attitude of quiet authority that shows he is friendly but expects to be obeyed.

When working around horses, move slowly and speak quietly to avoid startling or upsetting them. If a horse acts nervous, pat him and talk quietly to him to calm him down. Horses pick up the attitudes of the people who handle them; if you want your horse to be calm, attentive, and responsive, you must behave that way yourself.

HOW HORSES LEARN

Horses and ponies do not think the way people do. They learn by association: they associate (connect) a stimulus or signal (something they hear, see, or feel) with whatever happens immediately afterward. In training, we teach a horse to connect signals or cues with certain behaviors.

In training horses, we use "reinforcement," or rewards and corrections. Positive reinforcement (reward) encourages the horse to repeat a behavior. Rewards can be food, patting, kind words, release of pressure, or best of all, a break from work. Negative reinforcement (correction) is anything that discourages a specific behavior; it is *not necessarily punishment*. It can be a word like "No" or "Quit," a sharp, disapproving voice, making the horse stop and wait, making him do something over again, or simply ignoring the behavior. Always think of correcting a horse's mistake, not of punishing him.

In order to learn, a horse must connect the signal or stimulus, his behavior (what he does), and reward or correction within a very short time: one to three seconds. If you are even a few seconds late in rewarding or correcting him, the horse becomes confused. Always be consistent in the way you give signals and in which behaviors you reward or correct. To allow a horse to get away with an undesirable behavior sometimes, and correct him for it at other times, confuses him. Furthermore, it undermines his training and respect for you as his handler. Good horsemanship and successful training require correct and consistent handling at all times.

CHAPTER 2

BASIC HORSE HANDLING SKILLS

Ground training is a most important part of horsemanship. Good ground training teaches obedience, respect, trust, and cooperation, and it helps establish a good working relationship between you and your horse. It can improve a horse's movement, help develop his muscles correctly, and affect his attitude and behavior under saddle as well as in the stable.

GROUND TRAINING AND HANDLING

Whenever you are in charge of a horse or pony, whether your own or one you are riding or handling, you are either training him, preserving his training, or spoiling his training. Proper handling is important for the safety of your horse, other people, and yourself, and to prevent accidents. Good, consistent handling makes it easy for a horse to understand what you want of him and to behave with good manners. It is also important in developing respect, trust, and clear communication between you and your horse.

SAFETY IN HANDLING AND TRAINING HORSES

To work with horses safely and to prevent accidents, you must have good basic horse handling skills. When training or handling horses that are new to you, you may encounter horses that are flighty, difficult to handle, or have poor ground manners, and even a well-trained, familiar horse can act up unexpectedly. *You must make a habit of using safe, proper handling procedures every time you handle a horse, without exception!*

Safety precautions and horse handling skills are described throughout this book (and in the three USPC *Manuals of Horsemanship*).

Here are some important safety rules:

- Keep the horse's nature in mind. Expect a horse to think and act like a horse; never expect him to think or behave like a human.

- Dress safely. Shoes or boots should cover the ankle, have non-slip soles, and be substantial enough to give some protection if a horse steps on your foot. Wearing your ASTM/SEI safety helmet when working with horses protects you against head injuries just as it does when riding. Wear gloves to protect your hands, and remove rings or jewelry that could catch on a lead rope and injure you.

- Work in a safe area that is clear of distractions or hazards (such as tools, other horses, pets, or distracting activities).

- Pay attention to your horse's feet so you don't get stepped on by accident. Stay away from the rear of a horse unless you are working on him; it is safer to be near the front than the rear.

- Be especially careful when inexperienced people, especially children, are around horses. In explaining safety around horses, be polite but firm to ensure everyone's protection.

- Use good judgment about your own experience and abilities, and don't try to handle a horse or attempt training procedures that are beyond your ability. Get hands-on help from an expert if you encounter problems and before trying new methods on your own.

GROUND MANNERS

Good ground manners are a matter of attitude between horse and handler. Each must pay attention to and be aware of the other; you must communicate clearly, and he must be obedient and responsive. Good ground manners make a horse safer and easier to handle, but they are also an important basis for all training because they teach a horse how to pay attention and learn from his handler.

A well-mannered horse should be taught to:

- Turn to face you when you come into his stall, and be easy to halter.

- Wait for you to lead him through a stall door or gate.

- Stand still, on a loose lead line, when you say "Whoa" or "Stand."

- When being led, stay beside you (even with your shoulder) without crowding, pulling ahead, or hanging back. He should move off promptly in a walk or trot, and stop when you do, on a loose lead line.

- Obey simple voice commands: "Walk on," "Trot," "Whoa," "Stand," "Over."

- Lift each foot easily when you ask him to.

- Accept gentle touching with a whip without fear or resentment.

Teaching ground manners requires awareness, patience, and attention to details. Work gradually to get him used to new procedures in small steps. Letting a horse make mistakes and then punishing him for them is poor training. If you are paying attention to your horse, you can stop him *before* he makes a mistake, and can reward him for doing well.

Above all, you must handle your horse correctly and consistently *all the time*. Careless and inconsistent handling is unfair to the horse and potentially dangerous. It lets him develop bad habits that will have to be corrected. This is the fault of the careless handler, but too often the horse gets blamed for it.

BASIC SKILLS

HOW TO APPROACH A HORSE

When approaching a horse or pony, speak gently to let him know you are there, and go toward his shoulder instead of straight toward his face or behind him. Let him sniff your hand; stroke his neck or shoulder rather than his face or head.

If the horse is tied to a fence or is in a tie stall, you may have to approach from the rear. In this case, speak to him first so he notices your presence. Then approach from the side, and say, "Over," putting your hand firmly on his hip and pushing him over to the opposite side so you can step up to his shoulder. Never duck under the butt rope of a tie stall; this places your head in a position to be kicked.

Approaching a horse safely from the front.

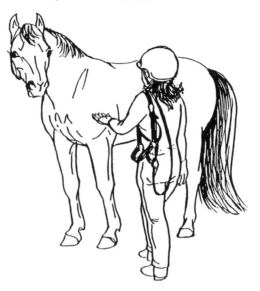

Approaching a horse safely from behind.

PERSONAL SPACE

Humans and horses each have their own "personal space," which extends out around them like an invisible circle. When someone or something enters your personal space, you notice and react to it. Both people and horses need to learn to respect each other's personal space.

You may invite a horse into your space by asking him to come closer, but don't let him rudely invade your space by crowding into you, nipping, or rubbing on you. If your horse crowds into your space, firmly back him up a step or two and make him stay farther back. Hand-feeding, playing with a horse's mouth, or encouraging him to nip or rub on your clothes teaches him to disrespect your space and gets him into trouble.

When you approach a horse (especially a loose horse), you must be aware of his attitude and reactions as you enter his space. Your attitude should be calm, friendly, and confident. A well-mannered horse will accept you entering his space and touching him, as long as you approach him sensibly. However, if you appear threatening, he may react defensively, in fear or resentment; if you appear timid or irritating, he might try to dominate you or drive you away.

LEADING

A horse must be well trained to lead in order to be safe to handle, to be jogged out for a soundness exam, to be shown in hand, to be trained to longe, or to be loaded in a trailer.

When leading a horse, always use a lead rope or shank unless he is bridled. *Never try to lead a horse, even for a short distance, by holding on to the halter without a lead rope.* The horse could act up, causing you to let go, or you could be dragged. You could get hurt, and your horse might learn a bad habit.

The following are used for control when leading:

- Lead snapped to center (chin) ring of halter (see diagram).

- Lead snapped to side noseband ring of halter (see diagram), for more control on a horse that tries to pull sideways against you.

- Lead run under the chin (see diagram), a more severe method which discourages the horse from dropping his head to eat grass. (Even more severe when a chain-end lead shank is used.)

- Lead run over the nose (see diagram), a more severe method, effective in controlling headstrong horses. (Even more severe when a chain-end lead shank is used.)

- Bridle reins (taken over the horse's head).

Attaching the lead line.

Attached to center (chin) ring

Attached to side ring

Under chin (severe)

Over nose (severe)

CAUTION: *Never* tie a horse with a lead shank over his nose or under his chin, or by the reins; he could pull back and injure himself severely. Don't drop the end of the lead or reins on the ground, where he could step on them and give himself a painful jerk.

Hold the lead rope or shank 6 to 12 inches from the halter ring with the hand that is next to the horse. When using a chain shank, hold the strap, not the chain, which can hurt if it gets pulled through your hand. The other hand holds the rest of the lead rope, folded so it won't drag on the ground. Never coil the end of a lead line around your hand; if a horse should spook or take off, the loops could tighten up around your hand. *Never* let yourself get caught in a lead rope or longe line, or fasten it to yourself in any way—that is dangerous!
There are two ways to hold the lead line:

- First method: Hold the lead in your fist with your thumb on top, 6 to 12 inches from the halter ring. To stop or turn the horse, give a brief tug backward or sideways.

- Second method: Hold the lead with your knuckles on top, 6 to 12 inches from the halter ring. This method may give you more control and, if the horse should rear suddenly, is less likely to injure your shoulder.

With either method, don't let your hand and arm hang down, making a constant pull on the lead rope.

To get your horse's attention, use short, light signals, not a hard, steady pull. Severe jerks, especially on a chain shank or the reins, are abusive and can injure a horse or cause him to panic and hurt someone else.

LEADING WHEN TACKED UP

When leading a horse that is tacked up, the stirrups should be run up and the reins taken over his head. Hold the reins 6 to 12 inches from the bit; your other hand holds the end of the reins, folded up so they can't drag on the ground. Never let the reins drop on the ground; if the horse steps on a rein, he may give his mouth a bad jerk and could break the bridle. Don't allow a horse to graze when he is bridled.

Holding the lead line.

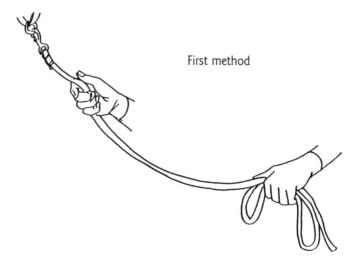

First method

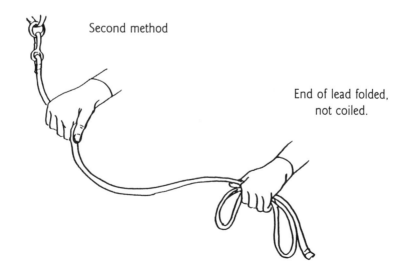

Second method

End of lead folded, not coiled.

Unsafe practices.

Holding chain

End of lead coiled
around hand

Never try to lead by holding
the halter without a lead shank.

Leading when tacked up.

TRANSITIONS IN HAND

Transitions are changes of gait and halts. Teaching your horse to make good transitions in hand, along with voice commands, improves his responsiveness and overall training. Handle the lead line with a light contact or a small amount of slack, never with long pulls or a heavy, dragging contact.

To ask a horse to move forward, you should be in leading position, beside his shoulder, facing forward. If you get ahead of him, you can't see or control him well, and if you face him, he may stop and pull back. Give a voice command to walk on, and move your leading hand forward, under his chin, as you move off with him.

To stop the horse, give the voice command, "Whoa," close your fist on the lead, and hold your hand still as you stop walking. The horse should stop when he feels the pressure of the halter. If he doesn't stop, give a short tug and release down and backward, and repeat as necessary until he stops. Long pulls do not work—this only teaches the horse to pull harder against you. To call attention to your signal, use a vibration (make your fist "shiver"), or a brief tug and release.

To ask your horse to trot, give a cluck or voice command and move your leading hand forward, under his chin, as you start to jog. Don't get out ahead of him and pull—that will make him hang back and get stubborn. When he begins to trot, look straight ahead at something and jog beside him in a straight line. To walk, give a voice command to walk, and close your fingers on the reins or lead as you slow to a walk; relax your hand as he comes back to a walk.

HALF-HALTS FOR BALANCE AND CONTROL IN LEADING

A half-halt is a momentary "rebalancing," which asks a horse to pay attention and balance himself. He should bring his hindquarters under him and "pick up" his balance momentarily. Giving a half-halt before starting, stopping, or making a turn or transition helps him move with good balance as he responds to your request. Half-halts can help to control a headstrong horse and keep your horse's attention on you.

To give a half-halt when leading, straighten up and rebalance yourself as you lift your leading hand in a brief upward tug, just enough to encourage your horse to raise his head and shift his weight back slightly. You must release the pressure immediately; a half-halt is a brief touch, never a long backward or sideways pull. If necessary, use a series of half-halts until your horse pays attention to a light contact or even a slightly slack lead.

Turns in hand.

Turn horse away from handler.

Turning on the hindquarters.

Turns When Leading

When leading a horse, turn him away from you whenever possible, instead of pulling him toward you. This keeps him from accidentally stepping on your toes and helps him move in good balance.

To turn, give a brief half-halt, then move your right hand out to the side, leading his chin away from you.

If you use half-halts to prepare your horse for each step, you can teach him to halt and turn on his hindquarters. This gives you extra control and lets you turn the horse in the smallest possible space.

Leading Freely at Walk and Trot

Some horses need to be taught to move off promptly and to lead freely, without hanging back. Start with the horse beside a fence, so that he has to go straight. If leading from the left, hold the lead rope or rein in your right hand, with the end folded in your left hand. In your left hand, carry a 4-foot training whip, with the tip trailing on the ground behind you.

Give a quiet voice command to trot, and move your lead hand forward as you move off. If the horse does not trot right away, tap him once on his hindquarters by flicking the whip sideways behind you. Tap just hard enough to make him trot, not enough to scare him or make him leap forward. You must tap him within 1 second of giving the voice command, or he will not understand. When he trots, be careful not to pull back; move along with him and praise him right away.

Teaching the horse to move out freely when led.

Bring him back to a walk and try again. If he trots on command, praise him; if he is lazy, tap him just enough to make him trot promptly, then praise him. You can use the same method to teach a horse to walk out freely instead of hanging back when led.

Another method is to have a helper follow the horse, giving him a little tap with a whip if he hangs back or doesn't respond to your command. The helper must be calm and quiet, must not tap too hard or scare the horse, and must be careful not to get within kicking distance. This method is not as good as working by yourself, as it draws the horse's attention away from you, his handler.

LEADING FROM BOTH SIDES

A horse should be taught to lead equally well from either side. This is an important step in preparing for longeing, and helps to keep a horse from becoming one-sided in his training. Because most people are more used to handling horses from the left side, it may take some practice before you can lead as well from the right side as you can from the left.

TEACHING "WHOA" AND STANDING STILL

One of the most important things for a horse to learn is to stop and stand still when you ask him to. This is important for his safety and for yours, and makes him easier to work with. He must learn to stop when he hears "Whoa," and to stand still on a loose lead line, without moving his feet, when you say "Stand."

Begin by practicing halts, using the voice command, "Whoa." Give the voice command before you tighten the lead line; use a stronger tug a second later if he ignores your signal. Your contact on the lead line should get lighter as you go, until he responds to the command, "Whoa," on a loose lead.

To teach a horse to stand still, say "Stand," and stand to one side, facing the horse, keeping some slack in the lead line; if you pull on the lead line or turn away from him, he may think you are signaling him to move. If he moves his feet, say, "No. Stand!" correct him with a backward tug on the lead, and immediately move him back into the same position. When he stands still, praise him, then move him off. At first, ask him to stand for only a few seconds; gradually increase the time until he will stand a minute or longer.

As your horse gets better at standing still, you can teach him to stand still while you move farther away (5 or 6 feet, then 10 feet away), and move around to his other side.

Teaching the horse to stand still on command.

ACCEPTING THE WHIP

Before you can train him, the horse must accept seeing a whip and being touched gently with it. Some horses need special help to teach them that the whip will not hurt them.

Use a stiff dressage or training whip, about 4 feet long. Standing next to the horse's shoulder, show him the handle of the whip; let him sniff it, speak to him kindly, and stroke him gently with it. Gradually stroke him all over his body and legs with the handle and then with the tip of the whip. Be gentle and patient, especially if he is uneasy about it, and don't tickle or irritate him with the whip.

If a horse is very nervous or has been abused, it may take time and patience to develop his confidence. Let him eat a little grain while working with the whip, to help him relax and associate this lesson with a pleasurable experience. If he is too nervous to chew, you are pushing him too fast. When he accepts the whip quietly, repeat the process using a longe whip, with the lash wrapped up. Then get him used to the lash, touching him gently. All this work must be done on both sides of his body.

VOICE COMMANDS

Training your horse to respond to voice commands improves his attention and responsiveness when you are leading or working with him; it also lays a foundation for later training, such as longeing. Always give a voice command a second before using a physical aid, such as a tug on the lead line or a touch of the whip, and give the command in the same way and tone of voice. (For more about voice commands, see pages 31–32.)

PARALLEL LEADING

Parallel leading is a special way of leading a horse, working from 4 to 10 feet away. It teaches your horse to obey you at a distance and prepares him for longeing. It also can be used to work him in hand over ground poles or similar obstacles.

Parallel leading is an important step in teaching a horse to longe. He must learn to move forward, stop, and obey voice commands when he is several feet away from you *before* he can learn to work at the end of a 30-foot longe line. This develops into parallel longeing, which prepares the horse for actual longeing. (Parallel longeing is described on pages 54–55.)

To begin parallel leading, start by leading your horse with the longe line in the hand next to the horse (as usual); carry the longe whip (with the lash wrapped up) in the other hand, pointing down and backwards. Gradually move out until you are about 4 feet from the horse's shoulder. Practice walking, trotting, and halting at a distance of 3 or 4 feet, then gradually increase the distance until you are working from 6 to 10 feet away. If the horse tries to turn in toward you, say, "Out," extend your leading arm out toward his head, and point the butt of the whip toward his neck. Practice leading, transitions, and voice commands this way on both sides.

To slow down or stop, use the same hand and rein aids you use while longeing. Repeated short squeezes (backward, toward his chest) act as half-halts and ask him to slow down or stop. If he does not stop promptly for a light touch, don't pull backwards or sideways. Instead, stop walking, hold your arm and elbow in one place, and give small "vibrations" with your hand, making your fist "shiver," instead of pulling. This teaches the horse to pay attention to a light signal instead of a pull.

To prepare your horse for longeing, introduce him to working on a large circle, about 60 feet in diameter, while you walk on a smaller circle on the inside track. Do this in both directions.

Parallel leading.

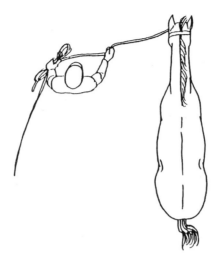

Leading at a distance of 4 to 10 feet.

Parallel leading, longeing position.

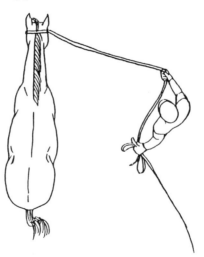

Leader has changed to longeing position.

(Both positions are used on both sides.)

LONGEING

Longeing is a way of giving a horse controlled exercise or training without riding him. The horse works in a 60-foot circle around the trainer, on a longe line about 30 feet long.

REASONS FOR LONGEING

- To exercise a horse when he cannot be ridden.
- To settle down a horse that is full of energy before riding him.
- To train the horse to pay attention to voice commands and the trainer's "body language."
- To develop the horse's rhythm, balance, suppleness, and way of moving.
- To improve the rider's seat and position (a rider is longed on a trained horse).

SAFETY PROCEDURES WHEN LONGEING

- Always longe in a safe, level area (preferably an enclosed ring), with good footing.
- Use the right equipment (see below), including protective boots for the horse and safe attire for yourself. Make sure everything is adjusted correctly before you start.
- Practice handling the longe line and longe whip before trying to longe any horse.

- Hold the end of the longe line in folds, not loops. *Never* coil or wrap the end of the longe line around your hand. Keep the longe line and any extra folds from dragging on the ground.

- Be careful when starting a horse out on the longeing circle, especially if the horse is fresh. Stay out of kicking range.

- Never longe a horse too long, too fast, or in small circles. This puts great strain on his legs and muscles and can cause injury, especially to young or unfit horses.

- Handle the whip quietly, and use the lash in an upward direction, toward the horse's shoulder, belly, or hocks. Don't wave the whip around.

IMPORTANT: To be safe for you and your horse, you *must* learn to longe a well-trained horse or pony with help from someone who is experienced in longeing, *before* trying to longe a horse that is green or difficult about longeing. You must have a safe place to longe and use the right equipment, or you or your horse could get hurt.

WHERE TO LONGE

The best place to longe is in a round longeing ring about 60 feet in diameter. You can also longe in a regular riding ring in one end or near a corner. Many horses are hard to control in an open field or in the middle of a large arena. It is easier to control the horse if the longeing circle is enclosed by a fence or barrier. You can use barrels, hay bales, or jump poles on buckets, but not jump standards or cavaletti, because they can get caught on the longe line or hurt the horse if he bumps into them.

There should be good footing, not hard or slippery. For safety, the gate should be closed, and no one should be riding in an area where a horse is being longed.

SAFE DRESS FOR LONGEING

Always wear gloves for longeing, to keep your hands from getting cut or burned by the longe line. Don't wear rings, which can catch on the longe line and cause injury. Safe footwear is essential; wear hard-soled shoes or boots that cover your ankles and have non-slip soles. Always wear your ASTM/SEI safety helmet, properly fastened, when longeing, especially when working with a young horse. This precaution can save you a serious head injury if a horse should kick or act up. Spurs should be removed when longeing, because they can get caught in the longe line and trip you.

TIME LIMITS AND CHANGING DIRECTIONS

Longeing is harder work than ordinary riding, because working on a circle puts more stress on a horse's legs, muscles, joints, and tendons. It also is boring, because horses have a short attention span. You must consider your horse's age, experience, fitness, and mental attitude when deciding how much longeing he can do. Longeing in hard, deep, or muddy footing, on small circles, or at fast gaits is extremely hard on horses and must be avoided.

When longeing, change directions every five minutes to avoid overworking the muscles on one side. Changing gaits frequently also helps. Use a watch or a kitchen timer to keep track of how long you longe in each gait and direction.

A horse that is out of condition or not accustomed to longeing should only be longed for 5 to 10 minutes (half the time in one direction, half in the other), with frequent breaks at a walk. The extra bending that longeing requires can make him sore if you longe him too long or too hard when he is not fit.

Horses that are fit and accustomed to working on the longe can be longed for a total of 15 to 20 minutes, changing gaits frequently and working half of the time in each direction.

CHAPTER 4

LONGEING EQUIPMENT

To longe safely, you must have the right equipment, and it must be in sound and safe condition, and correctly adjusted to fit your horse.

Longe Line (or Longe): A line made of flat cotton webbing 1 to 2 inches wide, or a half-inch round cotton or Dacron line, with a swivel snap or buckle on one end, *not* a chain. Don't use narrow, lightweight nylon lines or tapes, as they slip and can burn your hands. If the longe line has a loop sewn in the end, cut it off so you cannot catch your hand in it. A longe line should be at least 30 feet long so that the longeing circle can be close to 60 feet in diameter. Never longe with too short a line, because working on too small a circle puts great strain on a horse's legs and muscles, and can injure him.

DO NOT use the type of longe line with a chain on one end. The chain is too severe, and the weight of the chain spoils your contact with the horse.

Longe Whip: Most longe whips have a stock about 6 feet long, and a lash 5 to 6 feet long, used to signal the horse. Some whips are longer, in order to be able to touch a horse at a distance of 15 feet or more. (To lengthen a whip, you can attach a 6-foot braided bootlace to the end of the lash, or replace the lash with a longer length of shock cord.) A longe whip should be light and well balanced so that you can handle it easily. Practice using a longe whip (especially an extra long whip) without a horse until you can handle it fluently with either hand.

Don't try to longe a horse with a short whip (dressage whip or driving whip) or use the end of the longe line as a whip.

Longe Cavesson: A special headstall, made of leather or nylon, with a padded metal noseband and rings to attach the longe line. This is the best headgear for longeing because it gives you good control without danger of hurting the horse's mouth. It may be used alone or with a snaffle bridle.

A longe cavesson must be adjusted properly so it will not be pulled out of position. The noseband should rest about four fingers above the horse's nostrils and should be fastened snugly, but not uncomfortably tight. It must be on the nasal bone, not the cartilage. If adjusted too loose or too low it is very uncomfortable and may interfere with control. The jowl strap must be fastened snugly so the cavesson cannot slip up into the horse's eye.

Longe cavesson.

Longe cavesson over snaffle bridle.

When used with a snaffle bridle, the longe cavesson is put on *over* the bridle. The noseband of the longe cavesson goes *inside* the bridle cheekpieces, to prevent pinching and to allow the bit to fit properly. The bridle cheekpieces should be lengthened to allow for the longe cavesson underneath. The noseband of the bridle must not be caught under the longe cavesson; it is best to remove it.

Snaffle Bridle: A trained horse may be longed in a snaffle bridle, without a longe cavesson. To avoid injury to the horse's mouth, this must be done only by a person who is experienced in longeing, with a horse that is well schooled to longe, and only with a snaffle bit. The reins can be removed from the bridle or twisted several times under the throat, and the throatlash buckled through them, to keep them from hanging down too low.

The best way to attach the longe line is to fasten it to the inside bit ring and the inside of the cavesson noseband. (This requires a longe line with a buckle end or a snap large enough to go around the noseband.) This puts some of the pressure on the noseband, instead of entirely on the bit.

Longe attached to bit and noseband.

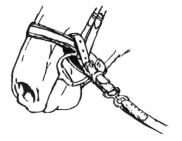

A more severe method is to run the longe line through the inside snaffle bit ring, over the horse's poll, and fasten it to the bit ring on the other side. This arrangement has the same effect as a gag snaffle, as it pulls the bit up into the corners of the horse's mouth and presses down on his poll. It must be handled carefully and should be reserved for situations which require maximum control, such as longeing a strong-willed horse that pulls, or for the safety of the rider when teaching a longe lesson.

Longe line over poll (severe; gag-bit effect).

When changing direction, change the longe line over to the other side.

Never attach a longe line to one side of the bit or run it under the horse's chin, as this can hurt his mouth. Never attach a chain-end longe line to the bit. (For more about longeing with a bridle, see page 67.)

Halter: Longeing from a halter is to be avoided, because a halter does not give you good control or let you give clear signals. Also, a halter may twist on the horse's head and slip up into his eye. Sometimes a halter may be the only head-gear available, or it may be preferable to longe with a halter over the bridle instead of attaching the longe line to the bit. If you cannot find a longe cavesson and must use a halter, it must be strong and must fit correctly. The type of halter that is adjustable under the chin can be fitted more accurately. If the halter tends to twist or ride up into the horse's eye, fasten a piece of leather or baling twine under the jaw from one cheekpiece to the other, to make a jowl strap. To longe with a halter over a bridle, put the bridle on first, and fasten the reins up (see below); then put the halter on over the bridle and reins.

The longe line should be attached to the ring at the side of the noseband, not to the chin ring. Attaching a longe line under the chin encourages the horse to twist his head sideways, and gives you less control. When changing directions, the longe line must be switched to the other side of the halter.

This method is strictly temporary, and the halter should be replaced with appropriate longeing equipment as soon as possible.

Protective Boots or Bandages: Leg protection should be used on all four legs when longeing, as a horse is more likely to interfere when working on a circle, especially if he is green, awkward, or excitable. Bell boots protect the heels of

Halter over bridle (temporary only).

the front feet, and splint boots or tendon boots can be used on the front and hind legs. Exercise bandages may be used to protect the legs, but these *must* be put on by an expert.

Saddle: When a horse is longed while wearing a saddle, the stirrups should be fastened up so that they will not come down and bang against him. (See diagram.)

Stirrups secured for longeing.

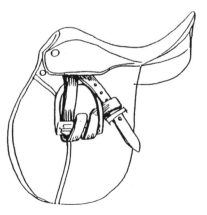

1. Run up stirrups as usual.
2. Wrap end of leather around iron, then fold upward.
3. Run end of leather through loop, then secure in keeper.

Surcingle or Roller: A surcingle or roller is a band equipped with rings for side reins, long reins, and so on. Used over a saddle, it provides attachments for side reins. Used alone, it may be used to provide an attachment for side reins or to accustom a green horse to girth pressure.

When used alone, a surcingle should be fitted as carefully as a saddle; a saddle pad is advisable. When used over a saddle, the stirrups should be removed. Be careful not to pinch the horse's skin between the girth and surcingle.

Side Reins: Side reins are attached to the girth or the billet straps of the saddle or to a surcingle, and snapped to the rings of a snaffle bit. They are used on more advanced horses to encourage correct head carriage and balance. Side reins *must* be adjusted correctly or they can cause great harm. (For more about side reins, proper use, and adjustment, see chapter 9.)

CHAPTER 5

COMMUNICATION AND CONTROL

The aids used to communicate with the horse while longeing are: the voice, the handler's body placement, the whip, and the longe line.

VOICE

To keep your horse responsive and attentive, keep quiet except when giving him a command. If you talk all the time, the horse will get confused and will not pay attention to your voice aids.

Your tone of voice and the way you say the words are more important than the actual words used. Give commands in a confident, cheerful tone as if you expect him to obey you, not as if asking a question. Each command must have a different sound, so that the horse can tell them apart. To encourage a horse to go forward or pick up a faster gait, your voice should sound brisk and should "lift" at the end of the command. To ask him to slow down, lower your voice and draw the word out.

The voice aid should be used first, repeated once or twice if needed, then reinforced with the whip or longe line as appropriate. Your horse should be taught voice commands while being led in hand, before you try to use voice commands on the longe line.

Voice Commands

The following words are commonly used to communicate with horses while longeing. Other words may be substituted, but always use the commands to which your horse is accustomed.

- To walk on: "Walk ON" or "Wa-a-LK," spoken firmly; raising the tone of voice on the last syllable.

- To walk from trot: "WA-a-a-lk" or "A-a-a-nd Walk," spoken slowly and quietly, but firmly, dropping the tone of voice at the end. The word *and* is used like a half-halt to prepare the horse when asking for a downward transition.

- To halt: "WHo-o-a-a" or "A-a-a-nd Whoa," spoken slowly and quietly, but firmly, dropping the tone of voice at the end. *Whoa* means "Stop and stand still," so to avoid confusion it is best to use another word (like "Slowly" or "Easy") to slow down without stopping.

- To trot from a walk: "Trot ON" or "T-rr-ROT," spoken briskly, raising the tone of voice and stressing the last part of the command.

- To canter: "Ca-a-a-n-TER," spoken firmly in two tones, raising the voice on the end of the word.

- To trot from a canter: "Tr-o-o-t" or "A-a-a-nd Trot," spoken slowly and quietly, as in other downward transitions.

- "Easy" or "Steady" (spoken slowly and quietly) may be used to calm an excited horse.

- Clucking with the tongue (single short, sharp clucks, not continuous clucking) can encourage a lazy horse to move with more effort. To be most effective, a cluck should be used in rhythm with the inside hind leg. If you cluck too much, the horse will stop paying attention. Instead of a cluck, you can use a short word like "Come" or "Hup," spoken briskly.

- "OU-u-ut," spoken firmly, may be used to ask the horse to move out onto the circle, away from the handler.

- "Good boy" (or any other appropriate term) can be used as a verbal reward. It should be spoken immediately when the horse does something well. (Don't use this word only when stopping, or your horse may learn to quit work whenever you praise him!)

- "NO!" This is a verbal punishment, to be used *instantly* when required. It should be spoken in a sharp, displeased tone of voice.

HAND AND REIN AIDS ON THE LONGE

When longeing, your hand on the longe line acts as your hands and rein aids do when you are riding. Neither you nor the horse should pull on the longe line; you should keep a light contact with each other and communicate with light rein aids.

To give correct rein aids, you must hold the longe line correctly. If your horse is going to the left, your left hand is your "longe hand," or "leading hand," used to give rein aids; the other hand holds the longe whip. The folded loops of the longe line can be held in either hand.

The longe line can be held in two ways: as you would hold a snaffle rein for riding (the longe comes out toward the horse under your little finger or between your little finger and ring finger), or as you would hold a driving rein (the longe comes out between your first finger and thumb). Hold the longe hand fairly close to your body, with a softly bent elbow and a straight line through your hand to the horse's nose. Your hand should be closed in a soft fist. Just as in riding, you give rein aids by squeezing or turning your hand, *not* by pulling.

For safety's sake, any extra line at the end of the longe must be folded into flat loops. These loops must not be large or sloppy, or drag on the ground where you could get tangled in them, and must never be coiled around your hand. You must be able to take up or let out the longe as necessary.

Rein aids given with the longe line must be coordinated with your voice, body placement, and whip, just as rein aids must be coordinated with leg, seat, and voice aids when riding. As in riding, rein aids are always given in a short "squeeze and relax," never a long, continuous pull.

Rein aids used when longeing include:

- Opening or Leading Rein: The longe hand moves outward and sideways, away from your body. This leads the horse forward and asks him to stretch his neck out.

- Direct Rein: The longe hand gives short squeezes on the rein, toward your elbow. This asks the horse to make the circle smaller, to bend toward you, or to stop pulling out away from you.

- Indirect Rein: The longe hand moves inward and sideways, toward your opposite hip, giving short squeezes. This puts pressure backward on the longe and asks your horse to slow down or stop.

- Giving the Longe: The longe hand moves briefly forward and out toward the horse's head, then smoothly takes up the contact again. This releases pressure on the longe for an instant. It is used as a reward, to ask the horse to lower his head, or to allow him to move out onto a larger circle. Don't

Holding the longe line.

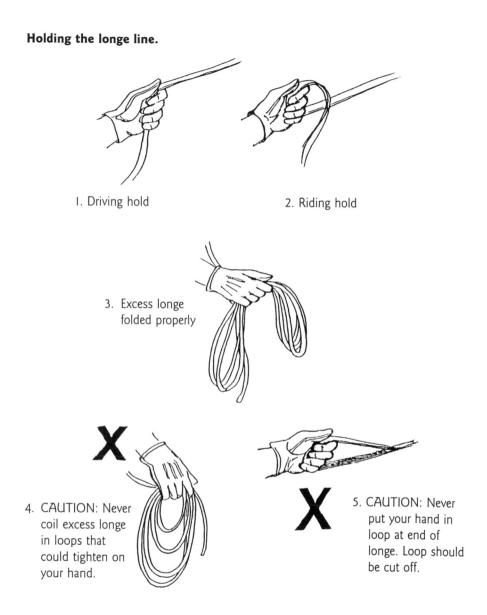

1. Driving hold   2. Riding hold

3. Excess longe folded properly

4. CAUTION: Never coil excess longe in loops that could tighten on your hand.

5. CAUTION: Never put your hand in loop at end of longe. Loop should be cut off.

lose all contact or let the longe line become dangerously slack; the horse could step over it if he turns in.

- Vibrating the Longe: The longe hand gives tiny "shivers". This calls the horse's attention to a light signal without pulling against him. It is very useful for halting and slowing down without pulling.

- Half-Halt: A half-halt is a brief call for attention; it asks the horse to listen to you, to rebalance himself, and to prepare to do something. To give a half-halt on the longe line, you coordinate all your aids just as you do when riding. Lift the tip of the whip or point it toward the horse's hocks to ask him to engage his hind legs; as you stand taller, give a short lift and squeeze of your hand on the longe line, and give a voice command. A warning word like "A-a-a-and," before a command has the effect of a half-halt, as it tells the horse that another command is coming.

Rein aids on the longe.

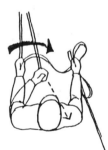

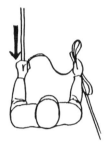

1. Opening (leading) rein: hand rotates sideways.

2. Direct rein: pressure straight back toward body.

3. Indirect rein: hand moves inward, toward opposite hip.

4. Vibrating the longe: hand "shivers" in place.

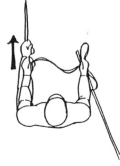

5. Giving the longe: hand moves forward, toward horse.

POSTURE AND HAND AND ARM POSITION

As in riding, "good hands" in longeing depend on good posture, balance, and shoulder, arm, and hand position. Good balance and posture make it easier to keep your balance, handle the longe line well, and longe safely. If you slouch or lean forward, you are unable to give clear and correct rein aids, and you can be pulled off balance by a resisting horse. Leaning back against the horse causes a heavy pull on the longe; this should only be used as a momentary defensive measure when a horse pulls hard or tries to bolt.

The long muscles of your back and the muscles at the back of the upper arm stabilize your arm and help you resist if a horse pulls. Your upper arm should hang close to your ribs, with a natural bend at the elbow. The forearm, wrist, and hand should be held so that the longe forms a straight line from your elbow to the cavesson. Carrying your longe hand too high is tiring and makes your touch stiff; dropping your arm too low pulls downward against the horse. Bending the wrist or pulling the longe hand inward causes a continuous pull and may teach the horse to pull against you.

CONTACT ON THE LONGE

The longe line should be treated as a rein, both in maintaining a light, steady contact and in giving rein aids. As in riding, rein aids should be applied as a brief change of pressure in a specific direction, NOT as a pull or jerk. It is important to keep the horse moving forward on the track of the circle in order to maintain the contact.

Practice letting out the longe (allowing it to run through your loosened hand) as the horse moves out onto a larger circle and taking in the longe (picking up additional folds) until you can do this smoothly with either hand. For safety, *always* keep the excess longe in folds, not loops that could coil around your hand, and never let the longe slacken dangerously or drag on the ground.

COMMUNICATING WITH THE LONGE WHIP

In longeing, the longe whip takes the place of your leg aids when riding. It asks the horse to go forward or move away from the handler, and can help maintain liveliness or impulsion.

The longe whip must be used quietly and tactfully. It is a means of communication, not an instrument of punishment. It serves as the primary driving aid in longeing, assisted by the voice, taking the place of the rider's leg aids. The horse should respect the whip but never fear it.

If you crack the whip or wave it around, the horse may become confused, frightened, and hard to control, or he may learn to ignore your whip signals.

Hold the longe whip with the tip low and the lash dragging on the ground. Normally it is pointed toward the horse's hocks or slightly farther back. If a horse is excitable or reacts too much to the whip, it may be held pointing backward (behind you). When you go out to the horse (to adjust equipment or when changing directions), the lash should be caught up and the whip turned backward, under your arm.

Holding the longe whip.

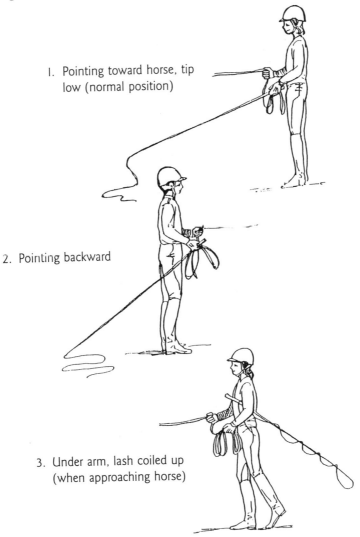

1. Pointing toward horse, tip low (normal position)

2. Pointing backward

3. Under arm, lash coiled up (when approaching horse)

The longe whip may be used in several ways:

- Pointing the whip: Most whip signals are given by pointing the tip of the whip toward a precise spot or by moving it in a gesture. The whip acts as an extension of your arm and emphasizes your gestures.

- Pointing the whip toward the horse's shoulder: Asks the horse to move out on a larger circle or stops him from cutting in toward the handler.

- Moving the whip under the longe line and in front of the horse's head: Asks the horse to slow down and stop. (This requires considerable skill, tact, and practice. Poking the horse or waving a whip around his head will surely upset him!)

- Running out the lash: The lash may be run out toward a specific point on the horse, keeping it close to the ground. This is accomplished with a quick turn of the wrist.

- Moving the whip close to the ground, with a forward rotating motion: Asks the horse to move forward.

- Touching with the whip: Touching the horse with the lash of the longe whip is a strong driving aid to send the horse forward. (This takes considerable skill and practice!)

The lash may be lightly tossed upward, run out to lightly flick the horse, or (rarely) applied with a stinging snap. This last should be used only as a last resort to stop a serious disobedience.

The lash should usually be applied on the barrel, at a spot close to the girth, where a rider's leg would touch the horse. If used on the hind legs or hindquarters, it encourages forward movement but may provoke kicking. Using the whip on the shoulder (to correct cutting in) should be reserved for experts because of the danger of striking the horse in the head or eye.

For safety, the lash should be kept close to the ground and applied in a forward and upward direction. Striking downward or swinging the lash wildly can cause it to wrap around the horse's legs or get caught on the tack or under his tail, with dangerous results. The lash must *never* be used near the horse's head, because of the danger of striking him in the eye.

- Cracking the whip: Occasionally an audible snap or crack may be necessary to send a recalcitrant horse forward. This should be done well behind the hindquarters and close to the ground, by moving the tip of the whip forward, then quickly backward. This is a sharp call for immediate forward movement. Use this only when all other signals fail, as it may upset the horse. If you crack the whip too often, some horses may learn to ignore all whip signals.

Using the longe whip.

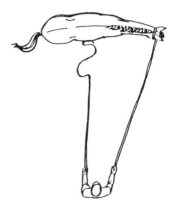

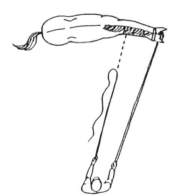

1. Pointing whip at hock.

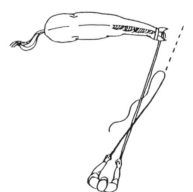

2. Flicking upward at belly.

3. Pointing whip at shoulder.

4. Pointing whip in front of head.

THE CONTROL TRIANGLE

When longeing, you and the horse form a triangle; you stand at the point of the triangle. The horse is one side of the triangle; your longe hand and longe line are one side, and your whip is the other. The point of the triangle (you) should be opposite the horse's girth area, just behind his shoulder.

If you move too far toward the *back* of the triangle (toward the horse's hip), the horse reacts as if you were chasing him from behind and might rush forward, kick, or bolt. When you move toward the front of the triangle (toward his head), he acts as if you were getting in front of him and cutting him off: he may slow down, stop, or even try to turn around. Normally, your body position should keep the triangle "balanced": be far enough back to keep the horse moving freely forward, but close enough to the front to control him easily. A small shift of your body in either direction will send your horse forward or slow him down.

The control triangle.

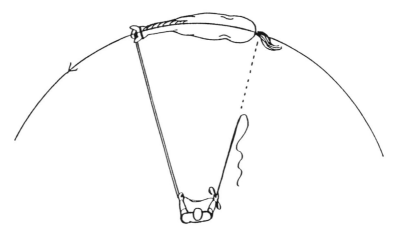

Adjusting the control triangle.

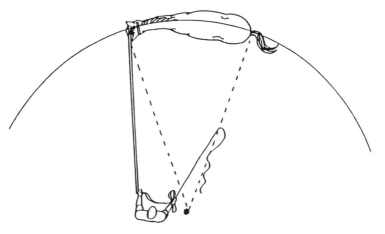

I. Too far forward; horse may stop or turn around. *(Dotted line shows proper position.)*

Adjusting the control triangle.

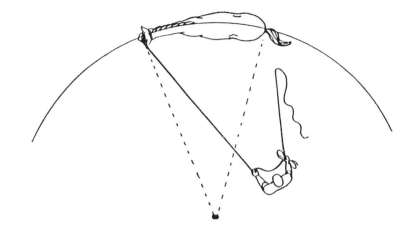

2. Too far back; horse may run forward.

Any change in the "control triangle" is a signal to the horse. Moving toward the rear sends him forward, as if being chased from behind. Moving toward the front tends to make him slow down, stop, or reverse. Moving toward the horse sends him outward on the circle and makes him more aware of your gestures and control, while moving backward increases the distance between you and the horse, and diminishes the effect of the aids.

When longeing, you must be aware of the "control point." This is a point on the horse (usually located slightly behind his shoulder) at which he reacts to your body placement and movements. You normally stay opposite the "control point"; getting behind the control point drives the horse forward, and getting ahead of this point encourages the horse to slow down or stop.

COMMUNICATING WITH BODY LANGUAGE

The way the handler uses his body is one of the most important aids when longeing. Horses often pay more attention to body language than other aids, because it is more like the way they communicate with other horses. Even if you give other aids properly, if you don't use your body the right way, your horse will have a hard time understanding you and will be harder to control.

Your body language (posture, gestures, and the way you use your body) conveys your mood and intentions to your horse. This is also communicated by touch, through your handling of the longe line and whip.

Mental Attitude: Body language starts with mental attitude. Clear intent is especially important. This means making a clear decision about what you intend to do and what you intend the horse to do. Your attitude of quiet confidence and clear, positive intent gives the horse confidence and encourages him to accept you as his leader. If you are impatient, hesitant, or indecisive, you convey fear, confusion, and a negative attitude to the horse.

In order to have clear intent, you must know what you are going to do and how to do it. It is important to learn and practice longeing procedures, to organize yourself, and to remove distractions before trying to train a horse on the longe.

Posture and Movement: Your posture and the way you move communicate your attitude and intentions to the horse. A submissive posture (eyes lowered, head turned away, shoulders rounded, backing away from the horse) conveys a nonthreatening or even fearful attitude. An aggressive posture (looking directly at horse with shoulders squared, head up, moving toward the horse) conveys dominance or even an attack. Normally, you should assume a neutral posture (balanced, relaxed, making eye contact with the horse) that is neither submissive nor aggressive. It is easier to get a horse to move in balance if you are balanced than if you slouch or lean. Deep breathing improves your posture and helps you project confidence and calmness.

Body language.

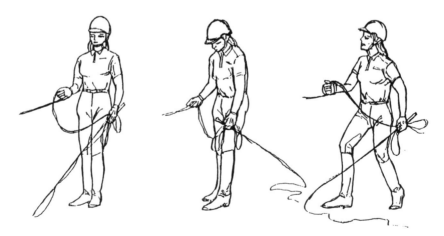

| 1. Neutral attitude | 2. Nonthreatening or submissive attitude | 3. Threatening, aggressive attitude |

Gestures (movements of your body, limbs, and whip): Horses understand gestures, as they use them in communicating with other horses. A gesture may be small or large, gentle or vigorous, which affects the horse's reaction. The longe whip serves as an extension of your arm; it accentuates any gestures you make. Some horses react more strongly to gestures (particularly whip gestures) than others.

Gestures used in longeing include:

- Pointing toward the hindquarters: Sends horse forward or asks for increased activity in hindquarters.

- Pointing toward a point in front of the head: Encourages horse to stop or reverse.

- Pointing toward horse's shoulder: Encourages horse to move outward on the circle.

- Moving arm and/or whip in a back-to-front gesture: Encourages forward movement and more activity in hind legs.

- Raising hand or whip: Calls for attention, may appear threatening.

- Lowering the hand and/or whip toward the ground: Diminishes threat; encourages relaxation.

- Shaking the whip: Draws attention to the whip; threatening.

Body placement: Your placement in relation to the horse is most important in longeing. Your leading hand and the longe line form one side of the "control triangle"; your other hand and the longe whip are the second side, and the horse is the third side. Your position, at the point of the triangle, should normally be opposite the horse's girth.

Good body communication makes longeing easier and helps a horse understand what you want. When you do it well, you will notice and react to small changes in your horse's attitude and movement, and he will react to subtle movements of your body. It's like dancing with your horse!

CHAPTER 6

LEARNING TO LONGE

To be safe, you must learn to use the longe equipment safely and effectively *before* you try to longe a horse. If you try to longe a horse before you can do it properly, you both could get into a dangerous situation.

PRACTICE WITHOUT A HORSE FIRST!

Here are some safe ways to practice:

- Hold the longe line with the extra loops of line folded correctly. Practice letting the line out and shortening it, without big loops that could trip you. Do this in both directions, and practice especially with the hand that is more difficult for you.

- Practice signaling with the longe whip, using a sawhorse or section of fence. Try to flick the lash so that it lands on the "horse's" hind leg below the hock, and on the barrel, just where a rider's leg would touch him, and on the shoulder. Do this in both directions, until you can use the whip easily and accurately with either hand.

- Practice longeing with another person acting as a "horse." (For safety, wrap up the lash of the longe whip and signal with the stock of the whip.) Your human "horse" can tell you if your longe line and whip signals, voice commands, and body language are clear. Trade places so that you get to experience longeing from the horse's point of view, too.

GETTING STARTED SAFELY

You should learn to longe on a horse or pony that is well trained and easy to longe, with help from an instructor. Your instructor will check the adjustment of the longeing equipment and should longe the horse first, to be sure he is behaving well. The instructor should stand behind you in the middle of the longeing circle and help you at first.

CONTROL AT THE WALK

To start a horse longeing to the left, stand by his left shoulder, facing forward and toward the horse. Hold the longe in your left hand about 3 feet from the cavesson, with the end of the longe folded correctly in your right hand. Your right hand holds the longe whip, pointing backwards toward the horse's hind foot, with the tip on the ground. Give a voice command to walk on, and lead him forward with your left hand as you move with him, staying opposite his girth. (If he doesn't move, point the whip toward his hocks and give the command again.)

Say "Out," and let the longe line slip through your left hand until he is a little farther away—about 6 to 10 feet. Stay opposite his girth and walk with him so he moves on a large circle about 30 feet in diameter, while you make a slightly smaller circle (this is called "parallel longeing.") Be careful when starting out, especially with a horse that is feeling fresh; never get into a position where you could be kicked.

To stop, say "Whoa," and step toward his shoulder. Quietly bring the longe whip forward so that it points in front of his chest (don't bring it up too high or fast, or you may scare him). When the horse stops, he should stay out on the circle; don't let him turn in and come toward you. Practice walking and stopping until he understands your commands and is going forward and stopping well on the circle.

Next, ask your horse to go out on a larger circle. Let out more longe line as you say "Out," and point your whip toward his shoulder. Now you will stand on one spot in the center of the longeing circle and turn on your heel, making a center point for a perfectly round circle. Don't let out so much line that it sags or touches the ground; the horse should keep the longe line slightly taut with light contact. If it becomes slack, control is lost.

Keep your horse "in the triangle" between your longe whip and the longe line. Stay opposite his girth area. If you get too far forward, he may stop or even duck back and turn around. If you get too far back, he may go forward too fast, and you may lose control.

If the horse tries to cut into the center of the circle, point the whip at his shoulder and say "Out." If he pulls against you, give a short tug and release on the longe line, like a half-halt. As soon as he responds, return to a light contact.

LONGEING AT THE TROT

When your horse walks and halts well from a walk, you may ask for a trot. Give a voice command to trot, and point the whip toward his hindquarters. If he doesn't respond, repeat the command and tap the whip on the ground behind him or flick it toward his hocks. When he trots, keep him moving at a steady pace on a large circle. After a few minutes, ask him to come back to a walk as you step toward his shoulder. After practicing walking and trotting, bring him back to a halt from the walk.

CHANGING DIRECTIONS

It's important to work both directions equally, to keep the horse from getting sore or becoming one-sided. To change directions, stop the horse, tuck the whip under your arm, (with the end pointing out behind you) and go out to him. In some cases, you may have to unfasten the longe line and reattach it on the other side. Lead him around in a reverse, and change the longe line and whip from one hand to the other.

Start off in the new direction just as you did in the beginning. Some horses do not like to change directions and might try to turn around. You may have to start with a shortened longe line and walk a large circle with the horse until he gets used to going forward in the new direction. Stay behind his shoulder point where you can control him most easily. When he is moving forward well, move out to the center of the circle as you did in the other direction.

LONGEING AT THE CANTER

Cantering on the longe line is more difficult than trotting because it is harder for a horse to keep his balance cantering on a fairly small circle. Don't expect a horse to canter on the longe unless he longes very well at the trot and has excellent balance in both directions.

To ask for a canter, use a voice command, and reinforce it with the longe whip if necessary. Some horses may have trouble keeping their balance at a canter on the longe line or may get excited and pull. You can help with short half-halts on the longe line and a calm, quiet voice command like "Easy," but don't do too much cantering, especially if your horse finds it difficult.

When longeing, a horse should canter on the correct lead. If he picks up the wrong lead, bring him back to the trot and let him get balanced before you ask him to canter again. Never canter on the longe line when the ground is slippery; he could slip or fall down.

Remember that longeing is hard work for a horse—much harder than riding for the same amount of time. Don't longe him too long or too hard, and be sure to walk for at least 10 minutes to warm his muscles up before work and to cool them down afterward. Always end a longeing session on a good note; ask your horse to do something he usually does easily and well, then halt him, go out to him and reward him with praise, a pat, and perhaps a tidbit.

CHAPTER 7

IMPROVING YOUR LONGEING TECHNIQUE

Good longeing is largely a matter of communication between trainer and horse, using body language, gestures, timing, tone of voice, and a consistent vocabulary of commands. This relates to the way horses naturally communicate with each other. Besides commands, cues, and learned responses, you communicate qualities such as confidence, relaxation, authority, energy, and awareness. Negative attitudes such as fear, anger, impatience, inattention, and indecisiveness are also easily picked up by the horse.

IMPORTANCE OF THE CIRCLE

Longeing is work performed on a circle. You can only evaluate and improve a horse's movement when he works consistently on a round circle of a given size. If he keeps changing the shape and size of the circle, his movement is inconsistent and you have less control.

In the early stages of longeing, the handler walks in a small circle as the horse works in a larger circle (parallel longeing). This keeps you closer to the horse, where your signals are more effective. In more advanced training, you pivot in the middle of the circle, providing a fixed center point for the circle.

GOING FORWARD ON THE CIRCLE

The first requirement is to establish forward movement on a circle, even if this requires parallel longeing or help from an assistant. If the horse hangs back, hesitates, or turns around, longeing cannot be accomplished.

ROUNDNESS OF THE CIRCLE

A longeing circle must be perfectly round. Horses may change the shape of the circle by cutting in or falling out. They usually do this at the same place (often toward the stable, or away from a spooky object).

Tips for handling circle problems:

- *Falling out:* Longe in an enclosed ring (preferably a round ring), or create a barrier (using safe materials) on the side where the horse pulls outward. Correctly adjusted side reins help keep a horse from falling out through the outside shoulder. Before he reaches the spot where he falls out, begin applying direct rein aids in rhythm with the steps of his inside hind leg. In difficult cases, the double longe may help.

- *Cutting in:* Before the horse reaches the point where he usually cuts in, send him forward by using the longe whip in rhythm with his inside hind leg. When he tries to cut in, point the whip toward his shoulder and say "Out." It may help to shorten the longe line and move closer to the horse (parallel longeing).

SIZE OF THE CIRCLE

A longeing circle must be large enough for the horse to move evenly and in good balance for his stage of training, but small enough for good control. The smaller the circle and the faster the gait, the harder it is for the horse to keep his balance and track correctly. Longeing on too small a circle, especially at fast gaits, puts extra stress on joints and muscles and increases the risk of injury, especially in immature or unfit horses. However, too large a circle makes it harder to keep control.

In early training, the longeing circle should be about 60 feet to 66 feet (20 meters) in diameter. As the horse's balance and strength improve, he may be longed on slightly smaller circles at the walk and trot (approximately 15 to 18 meters in diameter). Sometimes when beginning the canter, the circle may be temporarily larger (25 meters) in order to esablish contact and balance.

TRACKING CORRECTLY ON THE CIRCLE

Tracking correctly (tracking "straight") on a circle means that the horse's hind legs follow in the tracks of his front legs. This keeps his neck and spine properly aligned and allows him to bend correctly. It also improves his lateral (sideways) balance and helps him "stand up," remaining vertical instead of leaning inward, and it makes him less likely to interfere (strike one leg against another).

Horses often move crookedly on circles. A horse may carry his shoulder to the inside, swing his haunches out, or carry his hip to the inside. Many horses bend their necks too much to the inside or the outside. To some degree, this is due to the one-sidedness that is found in all horses. This problem must be addressed in order to strengthen and supple the horse, and develop his ability to move correctly in both directions. Allow the horse to establish a round, accurate track of the circle in a slow or even lazy rhythm before asking for engagement or more forward movement. Only when the horse is secure on the longeing circle can you improve his straightness in tracking.

Tracking on circle.

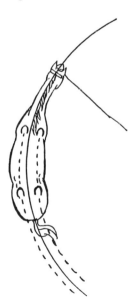

1. Tracking correctly on circle: hind feet follow in tracks of front feet.

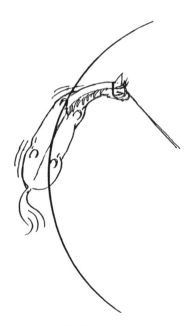

2. Incorrect: stiff; haunches swinging out; running through outside shoulder; overbending neck—"rubber neck."

Tips to improve tracking straight on the longeing circle:

- Correctly fitted side reins discourage a horse from looking out of the circle, bending his neck too much to either side, or running out through his shoulder.

- Longe on a large enough circle (approximately 20 meters). Too small a circle makes crookedness worse.

- Use the longe whip to encourage the horse to engage (reach farther forward with) his inside hind leg at each stride. Crookedness is often related to poor engagement of the inside hind leg.

- Keep the speed slow and the rhythm and tempo steady. If a horse leans inward instead of staying vertical or "standing up" and tracking properly, he is going too fast for the size of the circle.

- Horses that swing their haunches out may benefit from work with a double longe, which helps to keep the hindquarters in line (see pages 68–70).

TEACHING A HORSE TO LONGE

Training a horse to longe (whether a green or unbroken horse or a trained horse that has never been longed) requires confidence, patience, and experience in training and handling horses, as well as in longeing. You will need a safe place to work (an enclosed ring with good footing); an assistant can be very helpful.

The early stages of longeing are of vital importance, as this is where you make your first impressions on the horse, gain his respect and confidence, and teach obedience to your voice. This lays the foundation for future progress. Longeing can be a great help in developing a well-mannered horse, as well as in strengthening muscles, increasing balance and impulsion, and bringing an unbroken horse into condition for riding.

LONGEING YOUNG HORSES

Longeing puts lateral stress on a horse's legs and joints, which increases with speed and on smaller circles. Young horses' immature bones and joints are especially vulnerable to injury from too much or incorrect longeing, or from accidents if the horse acts up. They are also more easily over-stressed mentally by too long or demanding training sessions. Work in hand and free longeing are less stressful and safer for immature horses than longeing too much or too soon. When longeing young horses, always use protective boots on all four legs, and keep training sessions short.

Foals should not be longed, as they are especially vulnerable to neck injuries if pulled violently sideways. Yearlings can be longed at slow gaits for short periods but must not be overstressed. Two-year-olds (and some yearlings) have nearly reached adult weight, but their bones and joints are still immature. They can be longed lightly, but it is better to vary the training program with work in hand, free longeing, and ground driving, instead of daily longeing.

EQUIPMENT

A longe cavesson is essential equipment for control and to avoid damaging the horse's mouth, along with a 30-foot longe line (*not* the type with a chain end), and a longe whip. Boots or bandages are necessary to protect the legs in case the horse makes mistakes or moves awkwardly at first. Later, you may need a saddle or surcingle, snaffle bridle, and side reins.

PREPARATION

Before you can begin training a horse to longe, he must have been taught good manners during ground handling, tacking up, and so on. He should be taught to lead from both sides and to halt, walk, and trot in response to voice commands. He should be accustomed to seeing a longe whip and being gently touched with the whip all over his body.

Introduce the longeing equipment first (during grooming is a good time). Adjust the cavesson, try on boots or bandages, and let the horse see and sniff the longe whip before rubbing it gently over his neck, body, and legs. Work patiently and quietly, and make it a pleasant experience. This should be repeated as often as necessary, until the horse accepts the equipment with an unconcerned attitude.

REVIEW WORK IN HAND

Using the longeing equipment, review and practice work in hand (as described in the first section of this book), including leading, parallel leading, transitions (especially halting), and responding correctly to voice commands. Work from both sides and on a large circle in both directions. Be careful in handling the extra folds of longe line; do not let them get tangled, drop on the ground, or coil around your hand.

PARALLEL LONGEING

When your horse works well in parallel leading from both sides, 6 to 10 feet away, you may proceed to parallel longeing. Move out so you are about 10 feet from the horse's shoulder, and turn toward him. Hold the line in the hand closest to the horse's head, and the whip (still pointing backwards and down) in the hand that is closer to his hindquarters, as when longeing. Practice walking, transitions, and voice commands in this position, while you and your horse move in a large circle. You walk a circle about 6 feet smaller than your horse's circle. As your horse gets better at working this way, you can gradually move farther away—first 6 to 10 feet away, then 12 to 15 feet away, and so on. Be sure to practice in both directions. This exercise gives your horse practice in traveling on a longeing circle while you stay close to him for better control; it eventually develops into actual longeing.

Regular longeing and parallel longeing.

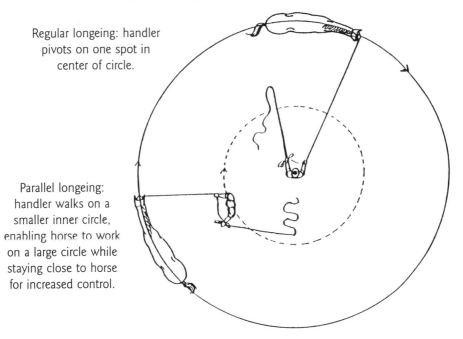

Regular longeing: handler pivots on one spot in center of circle.

Parallel longeing: handler walks on a smaller inner circle, enabling horse to work on a large circle while staying close to horse for increased control.

Beginning Longeing (with Assistant)

The easiest way to begin longeing a green horse is to work with an assistant. (The assistant must be an experienced horseperson who can lead correctly and who will follow directions.) The assistant can help give the horse confidence and prevent mistakes, while helping to establish control. However, one drawback is that the horse's attention may be divided between the assistant and the trainer, instead of on the trainer alone.

The assistant's job is to keep the horse on the track of the circle and help the trainer in any way necessary. This must be done as unobtrusively as possible, without distracting the horse's attention from the trainer's signals. The assistant never speaks to the horse but may give the horse a reward (a tidbit) when directed to do so. Eventually, the assistant "fades away" by doing less and moving farther from the horse, until the horse is longed entirely by the trainer.

The assistant leads the horse from the outside of the circle, using a lead line attached to the same ring on the cavesson as the longe line. (If the horse tries to turn into the circle, the assistant may walk on the inside.) The trainer stands at the center of the circle, creating a fixed center point for the horse to move around. One advantage of this method is that from the beginning, it teaches the horse to work on a round circle with the trainer at the center.

To move the horse forward, the trainer should give the voice command "Walk on," and point the whip at the horse's hocks. If necessary, repeat the command and the gesture with the whip. The assistant should move forward with the horse, keeping the lead loose; if the horse does not understand, the assistant leads him forward. When halting, the trainer should give the voice command "Whoa," step slightly forward (opposite the horse's neck), and quietly move the whip forward so that it points to a spot in front of the horse's head. When the command "Whoa" is given, the assistant simply stops walking; if the horse continues to move, he runs into the pressure of the assistant's lead line and the longe line. By walking on the outside of the circle, the assistant can keep the horse from turning in or out. (Some horses work better with the assistant on the inside. However, it is easier for the horse to see the trainer's signals when the assistant is on the outside.)

Practice walking and halting at various places on the circle, with the trainer giving all voice commands and words of praise. When the horse responds consistently to voice commands without help from the assistant, the lead line may be tied around the horse's neck, and the assistant walks alongside without touching the lead unless it is necessary to make a correction. When the horse responds correctly and consistently to the trainer's commands, the lead line may be removed and the assistant is no longer needed.

Practice longeing at a walk, halting, and walking on in both directions, with the assistant and eventually with the assistant "fading away." Keep the training sessions short (10 to 15 minutes) to avoid going beyond the horse's short attention span. Because the best reward is stopping work, always end the lesson with something that the horse does well.

Once the horse has learned to walk, halt, and move forward on the circle without an assistant, he can be introduced to trotting and further longe work as described below.

Beginning longeing with assistant on outside.

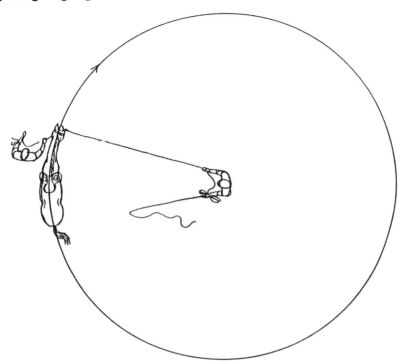

BEGINNING LONGEING
(SINGLE HANDLER)

If you don't have an assistant, or if you prefer to work by yourself, you can teach a horse to longe by progressing from parallel leading to parallel longeing, and eventually to true longeing. Without the help of an assistant, it is even more important to work in an enclosed area of suitable size (ideally, a round pen or longe ring about 60 feet in diameter).

Begin by parallel leading (leading from a distance of 4 to 10 feet), walking a circle of a size that results in the horse moving on a 60-foot circle. Practice halting and walking on, using the voice commands described above. Then move out to a distance of 10 to 15 feet and switch to the position for parallel longeing (see diagram on page 20). In this position, you can point or gesture with the whip more effectively to keep the horse moving forward on the 60-foot circle.

When longeing a green horse, it helps to stay slightly behind the "control point" to keep him moving forward. (See "control point," page 41.)

When the horse moves forward on the circle easily for several revolutions, prepare to halt. Move forward, ahead of the control point, and quietly move the whip so that it points at a spot in front of the horse's head, as you give the command, "Whoa." Keep the whip low and quiet, and omit the whip gesture if it worries the horse. If the horse does not stop, guide him straight into the wall or a corner so that he has to halt without turning. Turn the whip backwards, under your arm, and walk out to the horse to reward him with a pat and perhaps a tidbit; never bring him in toward you to halt him or he may learn to turn in whenever he wants to stop working.

You can gradually let out the longe and move farther away, but you will probably need to continue parallel longeing with a shortened longe line for a while in order to stay close enough for good control. Walk a circle that is round and large enough to keep the horse working on a 60-foot circle. Remember that your goal is to be able to longe from a fixed point at the center of a perfect circle; parallel longeing and walking a smaller circle are intermediate steps which should lead you and your horse to correct longeing.

LONGEING AT THE TROT

When the horse walks on and halts promptly and consistently in response to voice commands, you can introduce trotting. Give the command "Trot," and point the whip toward his hocks, or give it a small shake if necessary. Repeat if necessary, and praise immediately when he trots.

Let the horse trot several times around the circle; if he is slightly tired, he will be more willing to walk when you ask him to. Give a voice command to walk, and move forward, slightly ahead of the control point, keeping the whip low and quiet. You can give brief, gentle "check and release" aids with the longe line, but try to use voice commands and body language, and avoid pulling on the longe any more than absolutely necessary. Pulling inward too much may make the horse turn in or bend his neck sideways instead of teaching him to come back to the walk on command. If he has difficulty in learning this, go back to the walk and practice until the horse halts more easily.

RHYTHM AND RELAXATION

The main goals for longeing at this level are simple obedience, rhythm, and relaxation. When a horse is calm, relaxed, and under control at a steady, even gait, he eventually will find his best working rhythm and tempo. This is the rhythm and tempo (speed of rhythm) at which his muscles work most easily, and he moves with his best balance and stride.

Some signs that a horse is moving with good rhythm and relaxation are:

- His strides become even and steady, and his speed stays the same, without rushing or slowing down. You can count in a steady rhythm with his hoofbeats.

- His hind legs are active, not lazy, and reach well forward under his body. However, at this level, he does not have to "track up" (that is, engage enough that his hind feet step into the tracks of his front feet).

- He stretches his neck and his back, and his back looks "round" instead of flat or hollow.

- He breathes evenly and may snort gently, while stretching his neck and back.

Moving with good rhythm, activity, and relaxation.

LENGTHENING AND SHORTENING STRIDE WITHIN A GAIT

The horse should be taught to lengthen and shorten stride within a gait, on command. To increase the stride, use a short, sharp "cluck" or a command like "Come" or "Hup" once with each stride, and point the whip toward the horse's inside hock as the hind leg swings forward. To slow down the gait, use a command like "Easy" or "Steady," and give short, repeated half-halt aids in rhythm with the gait. It may also help to push the horse outward toward the corner or wall, or to move him in on a slightly smaller circle, just enough to encourage him to shorten his stride a little. Praise him immediately when he responds even a little. At first, the horse will probably slow down or speed up the tempo when asked for a change of speed. With practice and correctly timed aids, he will learn to lengthen and shorten his stride instead of simply speeding up or slowing down.

CANTERING ON THE LONGE

Don't try to canter a green horse on the longe until he is working well at the trot (see "Improving the Canter," Page 78).

To ask for a canter, shorten the longe and go back to parallel longeing, but walk a circle of a size that lets the horse move on a circle slightly smaller than 20 meters. Prepare the horse with repeated trot–walk and walk–trot transitions. Give a voice command such as, "Can-TER," and make a circular gesture with the whip, moving it forward and upward toward his stifle. As he strikes off into canter, allow him to move outward onto a 20-meter circle or a somewhat larger circle if necessary. Praise him immediately if he canters, and encourage him to keep cantering, even if only for a few strides.

If the horse has difficulty taking up the canter, do not try to drive him into a canter by making him trot faster. This produces a rushing, unbalanced trot, from which it is almost impossible to canter correctly. Running is not the same as impulsion, and chasing the horse faster will only make him agitated and unbalanced. Instead, develop better balance and impulsion through repeated walk–trot transitions, then try the canter depart again.

One way to overcome this problem is to longe the horse over a single ground pole or a small jump. This often causes him to land cantering in the correct lead. As he canters on, shift the circle slightly, to avoid jumping the obstacle again.

Cantering on the wrong lead is usually a sign of poor balance (it also may be caused by the trainer pulling the horse's head inward as he begins the canter). If the wrong lead is caused by a momentary lapse of balance or a mistaken signal, bring the horse back to a better balanced trot or walk, and try again. Do not allow him to continue on the wrong lead. Do not try to make him change leads without first bringing him back to a balanced trot. Cantering only on one lead is a sign of one-sidedness. A one-sided horse needs more suppling work at the trot in his difficult direction.

Cantering disunited (on one lead in the front legs and the other in the hind legs) often happens when a horse is too much on the forehand or when his head is pulled inward. As his hind legs swing to the outside, he is likely to go disunited. (This can also happen when a horse tries to execute a flying change and fails.) A disunited horse should be brought back to the trot and rebalanced before cantering again. He needs more work on tracking correctly, and on "standing up" (remaining vertical and bending instead of leaning inward).

ADVANCED LONGEING TECHNIQUES AND USE OF SIDE REINS

Side reins are reins attached from the bit to the saddle, girth, or a surcingle. They are used for limbering-up exercises, to help a horse find contact with the bit, to influence the position of the head and neck, and to develop self-carriage in a comfortable frame. The horse learns to yield or "give" to the bit and side reins, and to accept the position they create. Properly adjusted side reins encourage a horse to keep his neck and spine correctly aligned. They stabilize the base of the neck, which discourages "rubber-necking," or bending the neck sideways too much.

CAUTION: Side reins are advanced training equipment, to be used only by experienced persons who know how to use them correctly. If used incorrectly, they can hurt a horse and spoil his training, or cause accidents. You should have hands-on instruction from an expert when you are learning to use side reins.

TYPES OF SIDE REINS

- *Solid side reins:* Made of leather or webbing without stretch or "give." Some trainers prefer solid side reins because they provide a positive connection to the bit. Care must be taken to avoid letting the horse lean on them or get behind the bit.

- *Side reins with rubber rings:* Rubber rings inserted in the side reins provide some "give," especially if the horse tosses his head. However, they add weight to the side reins.

- *Elastic end side reins:* Elastic ends allow more stretch than rubber rings, making for a lighter and more elastic contact with the bit. While these may be useful for extremely sensitive horses, many trainers believe they encourage horses to pull.

Types of side reins.

1. Solid side reins
2. Elastic end side reins
3. Side reins with rubber rings

ADJUSTMENT OF SIDE REINS

Side reins must be adjusted correctly for their purpose and for the horse's level of training. They should not be used in the walk, as they may inhibit the balancing gestures of the horse's neck, shorten his stride, and spoil his walk. During warmup, side reins should be adjusted quite long if used at all, so that they do not inhibit the horse's ability to stretch his neck and back. Side reins must never be shortened so much that the horse is forced to retract his neck or to carry his face behind the vertical.

- *Normal side reins* are adjusted so that the horse makes contact with the bit when his head and neck are in a normal position for his conformation and level of training. His face should be about one hand's breadth in front of the vertical.

Adjustment of side reins.

1. Normal adjustment: horse makes contact with bit when face is about 4 inches in front of vertical; head at normal level.

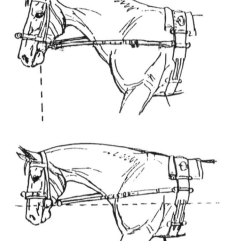

2. Longer adjustment (green horse): contact with face about 4 inches in front of vertical; mouth level with point of shoulder.

3. Shorter adjustment (advanced horses only): contact with face nearly vertical; mouth level with point of hip.

4. Incorrect: side reins too short, face behind vertical, overbent with neck shortened.

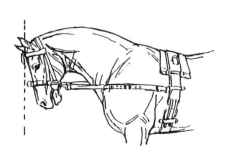

- *Longer side reins* are used in the early stages of training. They are adjusted so that the horse can stretch his neck and lower his head, and so that he makes contact with the bit when his mouth is approximately on a level with the point of his shoulder.

- *Shorter side reins* are adjusted to maintain contact when the horse works in a shorter frame in collected gaits, with his face at or near the vertical. They are used only for advanced horses, and only for short periods of concentrated work. Shorter side reins do not *create* collection; instead, they are adjusted to conform to the horse's increased ability to shift his balance to the rear, lower his haunches, and stay collected.

Both side reins should be of equal length. Some trainers make the inside side rein slightly shorter. This makes the horse appear to bend, but instead may encourage him to fall out through the outside shoulder and to overbend laterally in the neck. This can inhibit the engagement of his inside hind leg.

Always adjust both side reins before attaching them to the bit. Fasten the outside side rein first, then the inside. As soon as the side reins are attached, the horse should move forward. Some horses, if forced to stand still with short side reins on during adjustment, may lean on the bit, get behind the bit, or become upset, even to the point of rearing.

Side reins are only for work in the trot and canter, and should not be used in the walk because they can cause a horse to shorten his stride and spoil his walk. Side reins must be used only after the horse has warmed up without them. They should be adjusted a bit long at first, and gradually shortened to the correct working length (so there is a little slack when the horse is standing at ease, with his face in front of the vertical). As soon as the trot and canter work is finished, the side reins must be unsnapped so he can stretch freely while cooling down.

CAUTION: Side reins must *never* be used when jumping, as they restrict a horse's use of his head and neck over a jump and can cause a jab in the mouth, loss of confidence, or even a fall.

SLIDING SIDE REINS (LAUFFER REINS)

Sliding side reins run from an upper surcingle ring through the bit ring and back to a lower surcingle ring on each side, forming a triangle. They should *not* run between the horse's front legs to the girth, as this can cause the horse to overflex, carry his neck too low, and get behind the bit.

Sliding side reins allow a horse to maintain contact with the bit in a range of positions, particularly as he lowers his head and stretches his neck. Unlike regular side reins, they do not tighten or loosen as he changes the position of his head and neck. They can be useful for horses that have too high a head carriage, are tight in the back, and do not know how to stretch forward and down.

Sliding side reins should be adjusted so that the horse can make contact with the bit when he carries his neck slightly arched, with his face at or slightly in front of the vertical. Early in training, they are attached to the middle and lower surcingle rings. At a later stage, they may be attached to the upper and middle rings.

CAUTION: Sliding side reins are advanced training equipment and must be used only by trainers who understand their proper adjustment and use, and have advanced longeing skills.

Sliding side reins.

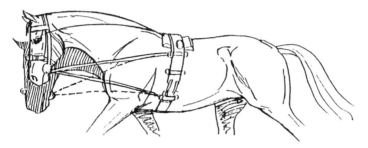

Sliding side reins allow the horse to stretch down while maintaining contact.

TRAINING DEVICES

All training devices, such as side reins and draw reins, are intended to develop a specific head and neck carriage. Training devices work by applying pressure when the horse deviates from the desired head and neck position, and reducing or eliminating pressure when he returns to it. In theory, the horse should learn to move in a correct posture and should develop the muscles that facilitate this way of moving.

Unfortunately, the use of such devices is not simple, and the results are not always good. A horse may "set his head," assuming a fixed head and neck position that relieves the pressure, but if he does this with his back hollow or his hind legs trailing, his balance, movement, and muscle development suffer. If a device is adjusted incorrectly or too tightly, the horse cannot find relief from the pressure. This causes tension, stiffness, and pain, and can ruin his movement and attitude. It also leads to defenses such as leaning on the bit, retracting the neck, overflexing, shortening the stride, and even violent resistances like rearing or falling over backwards. Incorrect use of bitting devices can cause muscle soreness, physical damage, or serious accidents.

Because of the dangers of these devices, they should be used only by experts who are extremely knowledgeable about horse training, movement, and muscle development. Any training device must be introduced tactfully, adjusted gradually to the point where it works best, and the horse must be longed correctly, with careful attention to rhythm, relaxation, engagement of the hind legs, and good movement. Most experts who are capable of using such devices without causing harm have no need for "gimmicks"; unfortunately, they are too often used by less knowledgeable trainers in search of a "quick fix." In such hands, they are frequently abused.

Some commonly used (and abused) training devices include:

- *Elastic poll pressure devices:* These apply pressure on the poll and the bit in a downward and backward direction, with some elasticity. They encourage a horse to lower his head and flex his poll and neck. Disadvantages: Although the "give" of the elastic makes these devices less rigid than some others, they can encourage a horse to overflex, flex behind the poll, pull on the bit, or become heavy on the forehand, especially if misadjusted or if the horse is not longed correctly.

- *Chambon:* A device which applies pressure to the poll and mouth when the horse raises his head; the horse is free to stretch forward and down. The purpose of the chambon is to develop the topline and back muscles. Correct use of the chambon encourages a horse to lower and extend his head and neck, while raising and rounding his back. Disadvantages: Chambons can cause soreness in the neck muscles. The horse may go on the forehand if not longed correctly. It takes weeks of correct and consistent work to develop the muscles and movement so that the horse carries himself and does not go on his forehand. The horse must be taught to respond correctly to the pressure of the chambon (by lowering his head) *in hand,* otherwise he may resist violently when he feels the pressure, even to the point of rearing and falling over backward.

The *gogue,* a variation of the chambon, can be much more restrictive, especially if misused; it should be used only by an expert. Pony Clubbers should not use gogues at any level, and the use of any restrictive device is strongly discouraged because of the potential for injury and abuse.

Training devices.

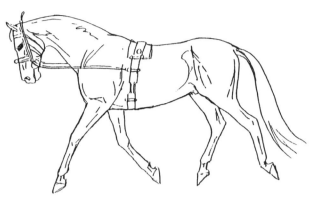

1. Elastic poll pressure device

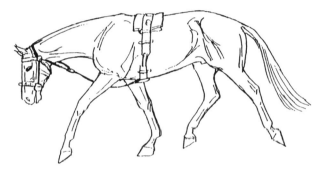

2. Chambon

LONGEING WITH THE BIT

For ordinary longeing, it is best to attach the longe line to the nose ring of a properly fitted longe cavesson. This permits good control without endangering the horse's mouth or interfering with the contact. However, it is sometimes desirable to longe with direct contact with the horse's mouth. This must be undertaken only by a handler who is experienced in longeing correctly, and only with a horse that is well trained to longe. Longeing a green or difficult horse with the longe attached to the bit can pull severely on the mouth, causing pain, damaging the horse's training, and injuring his mouth.

There are two methods of attaching the longe to the bit. The longe must be unfastened and changed to the inside whenever you change directions.

Longe Attached to Bit and Noseband

The safest method for the horse's mouth is to fasten the longe to the inside bit ring and to attach it to the side of the noseband (see diagram on page 27). This permits direct contact with the bit, while preventing the bit from being pulled sideways through the mouth. This method also transfers some of the pressure to the noseband, instead of to the bit alone. It can be used with a regular cavesson, flash noseband, or dropped noseband. It requires a longe line with a buckle end, or a snap end large enough to encompass the noseband as well as the bit ring.

Longe over Poll (Gag-Bit Effect)

The longe is run through the inside bit ring (from outside to inside), over the poll, and fastened to the bit ring on the opposite side (see diagram on page 28).

CAUTION: This arrangement acts as a gag bit, pulling the bit upward into the corners of the mouth and pressing against the poll. It is quite severe and must be handled carefully to avoid injury to the mouth.

This method is used when maximum control is needed, for example, when longeing a strong-willed horse that pulls or when safe control is essential, as when giving a longe lesson. It must only be used by a handler who is expert at longeing and has excellent hands.

- *Do not* run the longe line through the inside bit ring, under the jaw, to the other bit ring. This draws the rings together, pulls on the outside of the jaw, and causes the bit to pinch and hit the roof of the mouth, making the horse uncomfortable, crooked, and resistant. (This also applies to devices that snap onto the bit rings, providing a place to attach a longe line.)

- *Do not* attach the longe to the inside bit ring alone; the bit can be pulled sideways, right through the mouth, which will injure the mouth and damage the bridle.

THE DOUBLE LONGE

The double longe is often used in preparation for long-reining or ground driving. It can be helpful in longeing horses that persistently swing the haunches out, travel crookedly, or turn in to face the handler.

CAUTION: Using a double longe is an advanced skill of training and horsemanship and should never be attempted without expert instruction and supervision. Before double longeing, the horse *must* be accustomed to the feeling of the pressure of a longe line around his hindquarters, croup, hocks, and tail, on both sides, without fear or resentment.

Double longeing requires two longe lines or long reins, a longe cavesson, and a surcingle or a saddle with a strap to secure the stirrups under the girth (see diagram below). For safety's sake, the horse's tail should be bandaged or tied up in a mud knot, to avoid catching the longe line under the tail.

In double longeing, the inside longe line is attached to the inside ring of the longe cavesson and runs straight to the trainer's hand. The other longe is attached to the outside cavesson ring and passes through the middle or lower surcingle ring, around the hindquarters, and back to the trainer's hand. (If no surcingle is available, tie a ring to the stirrup or girth at shoulder height.) When changing direction, the horse must be stopped and both longe lines reattached in the inside and outside position.

CAUTION: The longe lines or long reins should not be fastened together, as this creates a dangerous loop in which you and/or your horse could become entangled. Be careful not to allow the extra folds of longe line to hang down in dangerously large, sloppy loops.

Start the horse off in a straight line, walking behind him as in ground driving. (In the beginning, an assistant may help by leading the horse.) After the horse has become accustomed to the two lines and has thoroughly accepted them, gradually move onto a circle, walking 4 or 5 feet to the inside, to accustom the horse to the pressure of the outside line against his outside side, hindquarter, gaskin, and hock. This pressure acts as the outside aids of the rider and discourages him from swinging his hindquarters outward. As work proceeds, the size of the circle can be increased and you can move farther away, until you are able to stand at the center of the circle as in ordinary longeing.

The inner longe is handled as usual, keeping a light contact with the inside of the horse's nose. The outer longe must be handled with a light, steady contact along the horse's side and around his hindquarters, to keep his hind legs following in the tracks of his front legs. The horse's head must not be pulled to the outside.

CAUTION: Don't let the outside longe drop too low, where it could become entangled in the hind legs, or lift it high enough to get caught under the tail.

Double longe.

Tail wrapped to prevent catching longe under tail.

CHAPTER 10

IMPROVING THE HORSE'S TRAINING AND MOVEMENT

Longeing is a good way to teach a horse to pay attention, respond to signals, and "learn how to learn." It provides a safe way to establish obedience, respect, and rapport, especially in difficult or spoiled horses.

LONGEING FOR OBEDIENCE AND DISCIPLINE

When longeing for obedience, you must read the horse's intentions accurately. You must recognize the difference between willful disobedience and mistakes caused by fear or misunderstanding, and you must handle each appropriately. Remember the "3-second rule": for a horse to associate a behavior with reward or correction, reinforcement must take place within 3 seconds or less. You must be prepared to reward or correct instantly, depending on the horse's behavior. One well-timed reinforcement can work wonders; rewarding or correcting even a few seconds too late will have negative results.

Work on one behavior at a time (for instance, moving forward promptly in response to a voice command). Be clear and consistent in giving signals, and be ready to act instantly. If the horse resists or acts up, you may need to escalate your corrections (for instance, from pointing the whip to snapping it, a light touch, or even a sharp crack). Be ready to reward instantly and generously as soon as the horse begins to move in the right direction.

LONGEING TO IMPROVE MOVEMENT

Longeing may be used to improve the horse's gaits, balance, and movement. Good longeing technique, along with careful observation and an "educated eye" for movement, can lead to improvement in muscle development and performance under saddle.

The following qualities are basic to good movement. They are progressive and should be taught in the order in which they are presented, as each depends on the foundation of the previous ones.

RHYTHM AND TEMPO

Clear rhythm and good working tempo come first. "Running" gaits are tense and quick, with short strides; too slow a tempo goes with lazy, dragging gaits and a broken or shuffling rhythm. An inconsistent horse that changes from slow to quick and back again cannot move well. When a horse finds the right working tempo, his rhythm becomes clear and steady, he can swing his legs freely in rhythm, and he breathes evenly. This leads to relaxation and better movement.

To improve rhythm and tempo, keep the circle round and consistent in size. Counting to yourself helps to emphasize the rhythm and helps you time your aids correctly. Watch the inside hind leg; the aids (half-halts or whip signals) should be applied as the inside hind leg pushes off and swings through the air.

For a tense, quick horse, longe at a slower trot on a slightly smaller circle (about 18 meters). Encourage a slower tempo with gentle half-halts in rhythm with the motion of the inside hind leg and quiet, soothing voice aids. For a lazy horse, point the whip toward the inside hind leg each time it swings forward, and use a stimulating voice command such as a cluck or the words "Come" or "Hup" to increase the activity of his hind legs.

RELAXATION, CALMNESS, AND LOOSENESS

Good working relaxation depends on both mental calmness and athletic relaxation or "looseness" of the muscles. This is only possible when the horse develops a steady working tempo. Mentally tense horses need to calm down and pay attention to the trainer instead of overreacting to distractions in the environment. You cannot teach the horse to engage more or use his body well until he is relaxed enough to accept your driving aids without tension or nervousness.

To develop calmness, the trainer's attitude and demeanor are especially important. Breathe deeply, use a quiet, soothing tone of voice, and apply rein aids with a gentle, relaxed touch in rhythm with the gait. If possible, longe in an enclosed ring, away from distractions.

Athletic relaxation and looseness of the muscles develop only when the horse warms up and settles into a good working tempo. Watch for the following relaxation signs, which indicate that he is becoming physically and mentally relaxed:

- The eyes are soft and the ears are not held stiffly.
- Taking a deep breath, like a sigh.
- Blowing the nose in a long, gentle snort.
- Stretching down with the neck and head and relaxing the back.
- Chewing the bit softly.

FORWARD MOVEMENT AND ENGAGEMENT

Forward movement comes from engagement (the reaching forward of the hind legs at each stride) and from the horse's desire to move forward. Good engagement provides impulsion or thrust; it also results in a swinging back that transmits power from the hind legs and can carry a rider better, and in better balance.

To move forward well, the horse must take long, powerful strides with his hind legs—*not* run faster with short, quick steps. A horse can only reach farther as the hind leg swings through the air, not when it is grounded and bearing weight. Point the whip at the inside hind leg as it pushes off the ground and swings forward, to encourage a longer stride in the same tempo. Be patient; it will take time for the horse to learn that the driving aids mean, "Use your hind legs more powerfully," instead of "Move your feet faster."

Do not be in a hurry to ask for tracking up (engagement to the degree that the hind foot steps into the track of the front foot) until after relaxation and a slow, steady rhythm have been established. These qualities take time to establish and must never be abandoned in a misguided pursuit of forward movement. Tracking up and subsequent engagement develop gradually as the horse builds confidence and strength.

Engagement and forward movement require work; a tired, sore, or lazy horse will move with short strides and poor engagement. Tense, quick, running strides, inconsistent tempo, and tension in the back prevent good engagement. A lazy horse may need to be enlivened with strong driving aids (stepping toward the hindquarters, snapping the whip, or touching him with the lash) to develop his activity.

Good and poor movement on the longe.

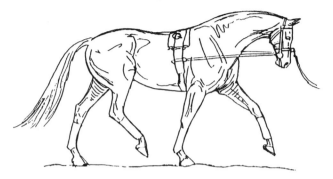

1. Moving well: round outline, tracking up, moving with good activity and engagement.

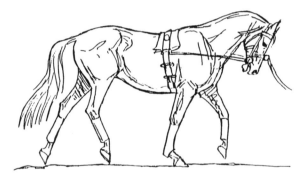

2. Moving poorly: hollow back, overbent, moving with stiff, constrained steps.

STRETCHING AND USE OF THE BACK

In order to carry a rider comfortably, a horse must move with a swinging back that is slightly rounded. This is caused by the engagement of the hind legs at each stride, the downward stretch of the horse's neck, and the use of his abdominal muscles. It requires a good working rhythm and tempo, relaxation and looseness of the muscles, and free forward movement.

Stretching down is a good exercise to develop a rounded, swinging back. To do this, the horse must accept the bit and stretch his head and neck down in a slight arch, seeking contact with the bit. Increasing the engagement of the hind legs (while maintaining the same balance, rhythm and tempo) encourage him to stretch down in a "rainbow" arc, with a round, swinging back and a softly rounded neck.

Stretching down.

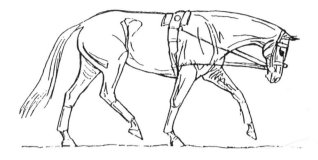

1. Correct stretching: round, well balanced, with good engagement and rhythm.

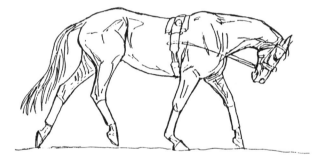

2. Incorrect: hollow, disengaged, shortening strides, slowing tempo, and leaning on the forehand.

Stretching down can be encouraged by the use of sliding side reins, which allow him to keep contact with the bit without tightening as he stretches. Use a leading rein in an outward and downward direction, while encouraging greater engagement of the hind legs by pointing the whip at the inside hind leg as it swings forward.

When a horse stretches correctly, he stays in balance and engages his hind legs—*falling onto the forehand is not correct stretching.* His head and neck should not poke stiffly out and down in a straight line, nor should the underside of his neck bulge. His hind legs should engage more, not less, and he should seek contact with the bit instead of evading it.

BALANCE AND TRANSITIONS

Work on the longe requires more balance than ordinary movement. Young and unschooled horses often have trouble keeping their balance on the longe line, especially at the canter. A well-balanced horse "stands up" or remains upright, bending around a circle. Leaning inward, pulling, stumbling or breaking gait shows that the horse is out of balance and going too fast for the size of the circle. Fear, tension, or lack of engagement may cause a horse to rush, which further handicaps his balance. Only a well-schooled horse should be cantered on the longe.

Balance on the longe requires good engagement of the hind legs (especially the inside hind) and appropriate speed for the size of the circle. The horse must learn to bring his hind legs under him and shift his balance to the rear so that the hind legs carry more weight instead of simply pushing it forward. This requires strength and coordination, as well as engagement, rhythm, and correct tempo.

To help a horse improve his balance on the longe, he may be fitted with side reins, adjusted correctly for his conformation and level of training. These discourage him from falling in or out with his shoulders and act as a passive restraint on his speed. The longeing circle should be small enough to discourage excessive speed, but large enough for the horse to track correctly and bend comfortably at his stage of training. Longe at a slow trot, using half-halts in rhythm with the inside hind leg, until he remains upright instead of leaning or pulling.

Frequent transitions are the best way to improve a horse's balance and strengthen his hindquarters. The horse must rebalance himself for each downward transition and push off with his hindquarters in each upward transition. Try trotting for 10 to 12 strides, walking for three or four strides, and trotting again, repeating these transitions several times in both directions. With repetition, the horse learns to stay in balance in the trot in order to be ready to walk, and to stay alert and engaged in the walk as he anticipates the trot transition.

Before a horse is able to canter on the longe, he must develop strong enough muscles to strike off into canter and stay in balance in canter on a circle (20 meters or larger). If he leans or travels crookedly at the trot, he is not yet ready to canter. More work on transitions, engagement, and tracking correctly on the circle will gradually develop his balance and strength. Before cantering a horse on the longe, make sure you have accurately assessed his level of training and the stability of his balance in trot.

SUPPLENESS, STRAIGHTNESS, AND LATERAL BALANCE

Suppleness refers to a horse's ability to shift his balance forward, backward, and laterally. It is not simply flexibility, which is the ability to bend the joints. While a supple horse must be flexible, a horse can become too flexible and "rubbery" (especially in the neck) if he loses his forward movement or is pulled sideways.

Straightness (in longeing) refers to the horse's ability to track correctly (the hind legs following in the tracks of the front legs). It also relates to his ability to engage and to carry weight equally with both hind legs and with both shoulders.

Horses are not naturally symmetrical; like people, they all have one side that is stronger and easier to use. One of the goals of training is to develop the horse as evenly as possible, to overcome this natural crookedness. This requires frequent changes of direction and extra attention to the correctness of the work on the horse's weaker side or difficult direction.

Correctly adjusted side reins, longeing on a circle of appropriate size, keeping the circle round, and frequent changes of direction are all helpful in developing suppleness. (See "Importance of the Circle," page 49.)

Spiraling in and spiraling out on a circle is an exercise to improve lateral balance and suppleness. Starting with a 20-meter circle, the horse is brought in on a smaller circle (approximately 15 meters) by applying a direct rein repeatedly, in rhythm with the gait, while taking in the longe line a little at each stride. Longe several times around the 15-meter circle, then send the horse gradually back out to a 20-meter circle by pointing the whip toward the girth at each stride (as the inside hind leg pushes off and swings forward), while letting the longe out. The horse should move forward and out slightly at each stride, not outward all at once. The exercise should be practiced in both directions, with emphasis on the horse's more difficult side.

IMPROVING ACCEPTANCE OF THE BIT

Longeing can be used to educate a green horse to accept the bit and to give to it, or to improve a horse with problems in this area. (First, make sure that the horse's mouth is comfortable and that he has no painful teeth.) The horse should be fitted with a smooth snaffle bit with a comfortable, moderately thick mouthpiece, a saddle or roller, and side reins of equal length. Don't overtighten the throatlash or noseband, as this can inhibit correct flexion and relaxation of the jaw.

Sliding side reins may be helpful for horses that are tense, high headed, or tight in the back; horses that are oversensitive in the mouth may do better with elastic side reins. Use a longe cavesson to avoid interfering with the contact or pulling on his mouth.

After warming up without side reins, adjust the side reins so that the horse can make contact with the bit when the front of his face is about a hand's width in front of the vertical, with his mouth at approximately the level of the point of his shoulder. Longe at a trot with a steady, not too fast tempo, and encourage the horse to take longer strides with his hind legs, without quickening or rushing. As he engages his hind legs more, he will stretch his back and reach out and down with his head and neck. If the side reins are correctly adjusted, the horse makes his own gentle contact with the bit.

It is particularly important not to overshorten the side reins or cause the horse to "set his head," retract his neck, or overflex. However, side reins adjusted too long make it impossible for a horse to make contact with the bit while moving in good balance.

Signs of progress include:

- Gently chewing the bit, which produces foam in the mouth.

- Stretching the neck and back, showing more roundness in the back, while continuing to reach well forward with the hind legs.

- A more steady and consistent, but not rigid, head carriage.

- Indications of relaxation, such as a rhythmically swinging tail, breathing in rhythm with the strides, and gently snorting or "blowing his nose."

- Developing self-carriage as a result of meeting and giving to the side reins.

IMPROVING THE CANTER

For most horses, cantering on the longe is more difficult than trotting, as it requires more balance, strength, and suppleness. Correct longeing can greatly improve the horse's canter work under saddle. It must be introduced gradually, however, and kept within the horse's capabilities.

Before cantering on the longe, the horse must longe well at the trot, tracking correctly and moving with good balance, impulsion, and correct bend. He must not lean or pull against the longe, or travel crookedly. He may be fitted with side reins, adjusted for normal longeing (face about a hand's width in front of the vertical). More advanced horses can canter with shorter side reins (face nearly vertical, mouth on a level with the point of the hip), but they must be able to maintain good forward impulsion and balance in a more collected frame.

Practicing a series of transitions (trot–walk and walk–trot) improves the horse's balance and impulsion in preparation for the canter. Asking him to strike off into canter from a walk or collected trot results in a better balanced canter than if he runs into it from a fast trot. The horse should strike off into canter on a circle a little smaller than 20 meters, then move outward, correctly bent, to canter on the larger circle. Give a clear signal that means "Canter," not a signal that could be mistaken for a command to speed up the trot. If he misses the canter depart, bring him back to balance in a walk or collected trot before trying again.

Keep the circle round but large enough for good balance at the canter (at least 20 meters). You may need to revert to parallel longeing in order to make the circle large enough and to stay closer to the horse so he is more aware of your aids. Longeing in a ring with a fence or a barrier supports your outside aids and helps to prevent the horse from pulling or falling out.

Emphasize the "jump" in each canter stride by gesturing with your whip toward the inside hind leg as it reaches forward. If the horse hollows his back, his engagement suffers, the canter becomes "flat," and it may degenerate into a four-beat canter. Too restrictive side reins, trying to slow the canter down too much, or cantering on too small a circle for the horse's level of training, can lead to this problem. (For more about canter work on the longe, see pages 47 and 60.)

CHAPTER 11

LONGEING FOR SPECIAL PURPOSES

Longeing can be used to exercise a horse in place of riding. Because longeing is harder work than it appears and is especially stressful on unfit or immature joints, you must assess the horse's level of fitness and keep the longeing workload within his limits. Twenty minutes should be the maximum for a fit horse; young or unfit horses should be longed for 10 minutes or less, increasing gradually as the horse's fitness increases.

Always longe on good footing, warm up slowly, and warm down at the end of the session. Work equally in both directions (or slightly more in the horse's difficult direction), and use a timer to keep track of how long he is worked in each direction and the total time.

In addition to exercise, longeing can be used for other purposes, too.

LONGEING TO SETTLE A FRESH HORSE

Longeing can settle a fresh horse or relax a tense horse before riding. This is especially important in teaching riding when a student's horse is too fresh to ride safely. It is best to longe with the saddle and bridle in place (with a cavesson and side reins added).

CAUTION: Fresh horses are likely to kick, so follow safety procedures carefully, and be alert!

Start out as quietly as possible (at a walk, if the horse will cooperate). If the horse is very fresh, it is better to allow him to trot slowly than to fight him about walking. Do not allow bucking and running, because it increases the risk of injury and because a horse should associate longeing with steadiness and good behavior, not wild, undisciplined behavior. Instead, emphasize developing steady rhythm and tempo, relaxation, and free forward movement. If a horse needs to run, buck, and play, it is safer for him and better for his training to turn him out rather than let him run and buck on the longe.

LONGEING AN UNFAMILIAR HORSE

When longeing an unfamiliar horse, your primary goals are to assess his movement, attitude, and level of training, and to establish a rapport that will allow you to work with him. Safety precautions are always important, but especially so when working with an unfamiliar horse. Be very careful not to get into a position in which you could be kicked, and treat an unfamiliar horse as if he were a green horse until you ascertain otherwise.

Before longeing, show the horse the longe whip, then run it gently over his body, noting his reactions. Practice parallel leading with halts and transitions to see if he responds to voice commands. You can then proceed to parallel longeing, then regular longeing. Note which direction is easier and which is more difficult, and be alert to keep him from stopping and turning around when working in his difficult direction.

As you longe, assess the horse's balance, movement, acceptance of the bit and side reins, and response to your aids and signals. Consider his temperament and willingness to cooperate with you.

Some categories of horses:

- *Well-schooled:* Familiar with longeing, supple and responsive, able to move correctly in all gaits, accepts the aids, and responds correctly.

- *Balance and movement problems:* Obedient but stiff, crooked, or unbalanced (usually more so in one direction). May not be able to canter safely on the longe.

- *Green:* Unbacked, or never longed before.

- *Problem horses:* Difficult attitude (tense, "hot," fearful, stubborn, lazy, and so on) or bad habits (balking, bolting, turning around, kicking, and so on).

LONGEING AWAY FROM HOME

You may need to longe a horse to settle him in a strange place or before a competition. Before you can longe safely away from home, your horse *must* be well schooled at home, and you should be able to longe him safely in the open.

At a competition, clinic, or rally, there may be very little safe space in which to longe. Sometimes the only available space is not level. Use good judgment about where you longe and whether longeing is feasible at all, given the footing and conditions. Do not monopolize the schooling area or longe in an area that is too busy to be safe. You may have to longe in a smaller circle than usual (if so, do less than usual, because the work is harder for your horse) or in the open.

Especially in the open, keep the work slow and emphasize steady rhythm, stretching, and quiet obedience. Keep his attention on you by timely use of transitions, voice commands, longe, and whip, and watch for signs of relaxation and loosening up (chewing the bit, blowing his nose, and stretching his neck and back). Discourage bucking and playing.

Don't overdo longeing, especially when warming up for a competition.

CHAPTER 12

HANDLING COMMON LONGEING PROBLEMS

DISOBEDIENCES

When dealing with a willfully disobedient horse, you must act with confidence, good timing, and a positive, assertive attitude. If a horse bucks or bolts, place one foot in front of you, bend your knees, and keep your shoulders back. Use short, strong half-halts and firm voice commands. A horse that kicks should be corrected with a sharp, displeased voice and a swift, upward jerk on the longe line.

A horse whose obedience is questionable must only be longed in an enclosed ring with no riders present. Don't allow him to drag you around! If the horse is too strong for you to hold, let him go rather than take chances with your safety or his.

Never longe a rider unless you are sure the horse being used is consistently obedient.

EVASIONS

The horse that does not go forward and the horse that comes in on the circle (often practiced simultaneously) are evading your control and the work of longeing. Use the command, "Out," and point or shake the whip at his shoulder, as you step forward on the line of the whip, then drive him forward from behind. Increasing or decreasing the size of the circle for one round may also help.

A more serious type of evasion is turning the head in and swinging the quarters out, sometimes swinging around to face the trainer. This type of evasion is more common when a horse is worked without side reins, which is a good reason for using them. The horse should be fitted with correctly adjusted side reins, with the outside side rein short enough to discourage him from bending his neck too much and popping his outside shoulder out. Send him forward strongly so that he cannot shorten stride, hesitate, or stop. In difficult cases, the double longe may be helpful.

If the horse succeeds in stopping, facing you, or if he begins backing away, follow him until he is stopped by reaching a wall or other barrier, then step back, opposite his hindquarters, and send him forward. You may need to shorten the longe, move closer to him, and move in a circle (parallel longeing). Horses usually try this evasion in the same spot, so be aware of any hesitation or shortening of stride as he approaches that point, and send him forward. Be careful not to get ahead of the "control point," which can provoke this behavior.

Some horses stop and whirl around, especially after changing directions or when longed in their difficult direction. Stop the horse and reposition him (lead his head around until he is facing in the correct direction), then send him forward. This action must be taken promptly and firmly, but not roughly; avoid "rewarding" the horse with a rest or release of pressure until he is moving forward again in the direction he should.

THE STUBBORN HORSE

When longeing a calm but stubborn horse (one that refuses to move forward, frequently stops, or has no respect for the whip), stop and analyze the situation. Make sure there is nothing nearby that distracts or worries the horse. Go back to parallel longeing, or even parallel leading, to establish the basic idea of longeing. Use the whip close enough to his hocks to make him respect it and move forward. Stay close enough to reach the horse with the whip, even if you have to walk a large circle.

If nothing else works, try having an experienced rider ride the horse on the longe line, applying leg aids each time you give a voice command.

THE LAZY HORSE

A lazy horse avoids the work of longeing (and therefore, its benefits) by putting forth the least effort he can get away with. It is all too easy to fall into a pattern of nagging so that you do more and work harder while the horse pays even less attention to you. Instead, insist on a prompt response to your aids by using the whip immediately when he fails to respond, as sharply as necessary to command his attention and awaken his energy. Shorten the longe and walk a circle (parallel longeing) so that you are close enough to reach him with the whip. It may be necessary to hit him once across the rump, hard enough to make him respect the whip.

Lazy horses do better when kept busy with frequent transitions and different exercises, and in fairly brief sessions.

THE BORED HORSE

Horses easily become bored with longeing, because of the repetitive nature of the work. A horse that suddenly becomes uncooperative may be bored. Keep longeing sessions short; keep the horse's attention by varying gaits, making frequent transitions, changing directions, and spiralling in or out. Longeing over a single ground pole can also restore a horse's interest. Try longeing in different locations, and avoid a fixed routine.

THE RUSHING HORSE

If a horse rushes or won't stop, check your body language and your handling of the whip; make sure you are not unknowingly "chasing" him forward. Keep the whip quiet and pointing toward the ground, or reverse it so that it trails behind you. Shorten the longe and move closer to him, walking a circle (parallel longeing). Move forward, opposite the horse's neck, and use voice commands along with repeated half-halts, timed with the swing of the inside hind leg. Making the circle slightly smaller may help slow him down.

To stop a rushing horse, move with him and use a "body block" or direct him into a fence, wall, or corner (which must be too high to jump), giving a voice command to halt just before he is forced to stop.

THE ONE-SIDED HORSE

If a horse longes well in one direction but consistently resists in the other, treat him as though he were a green horse when longeing in his difficult direction, asking for only a little work at a time. When he becomes more comfortable longeing in his difficult direction, he should be worked *slightly longer* on that side to achieve equal suppleness on both sides.

A one-sided horse should be checked by a veterinarian to determine whether lameness, soreness, or faulty vision in one eye might be the cause of his difficulty.

THE FRIGHTENED OR DIFFICULT HORSE

Do not attempt to longe a really frightened or extremely difficult horse. If a longeing session degenerates into a rodeo performance, the danger of injury to both you and the horse is too great, and the horse will learn nothing of value. Go back to work in hand to establish trust, obedience, and safe control.

PROBLEMS CAUSED BY THE HANDLER

Many longeing problems are caused by the handler's mistakes or lack of skill. In these cases, the solution is to improve yourself. Some common handler errors are:

- Not teaching control first, especially "Whoa" or "Halt."
- Nagging the horse.
- Incorrect technique with longe or whip.
- Dwelling too long on one thing or an exercise.
- Poor timing; misreading the horse.
- Weak and indefinite voice commands.
- Constant talking.
- Becoming distracted; not paying attention.

CHAPTER 13

LONGEING THE RIDER

Longe lessons can be very beneficial for riders of all levels. However, it takes a great deal of knowledge and experience to longe a horse and teach a rider at the same time. The instructor must longe the horse safely and correctly, and produce the right kind of movement for the rider. At the same time, he or she must be able to evaluate the student's riding, teach the proper exercises, and address his needs (physical and mental), while keeping the work within the capabilities of both horse and rider. Because the rider's safety is entirely in the hands of the instructor, safety must be the number one consideration and the instructor must be alert, aware, and conscientious about following safe and correct longeing procedures.

Longe lessons allow riders to concentrate on improving their riding without having to control the horse. Essentially, longe lessons are used to:

- Build confidence.

- Improve suppleness, eliminate stiffness, and help the rider follow the horse's movements more accurately.

- Improve a rider's balance, security, and correct position.

- Develop a secure, correct, supple, and independent seat, from which the rider can apply his aids correctly and easily.

Longe lessons can be useful for students of all levels, as long as the instructor is sufficiently skilled, the horse is suitable, and the length and demands of the lesson are appropriate. Beginning riders are often started on the longe line, but the instructor must be especially careful to make this a safe and positive experience.

The instructor must always pay attention to the following:

- *Confidence:* Persisting in spite of the rider's fear and tension prevents progress and leads to soreness, bad experiences, greater fear, and potentially dangerous situations. If a student is afraid or tense, go back to easier work!

- *Balance:* The rider needs to find a correct balance; weight must be evenly distributed over both seat bones and a balanced pelvis. If the rider tips forward, backward, or off to one side, especially in transitions, go back to a slower pace and reestablish correct balance.

- *Suppleness:* Suppleness is related to balance and confidence. Loss of balance will cause a rider to tighten muscles or grip in an effort to stay on; fear or lack of confidence will cause stiffness. Stiffness can disrupt balance.

Whenever a student begins to lose confidence, balance, or suppleness, immediately go back to a slower pace, an easier exercise, or even halt in order to reestablish correct fundamentals.

Be aware of the rider's level of fitness and fatigue; longe exercises are tiring. Many short repetitions with brief rest periods are better than prolonging an exercise to the point of exhaustion. (This also applies to the horse, who must not be longed too long in one direction or too long or hard in any session.) Longeing a rider until he "gets it" is very hard on both horse and rider, and it is unsafe. Afterward, the rider usually doesn't know what was done correctly.

The importance of teaching simple fundamentals correctly cannot be overstressed. Whatever the student practices, right or wrong, will become a habit. Remember, only *perfect* practice makes perfect!

REQUIREMENTS FOR LONGE LESSONS

- Safe longeing area with good footing, preferably an enclosed ring, with a minimum of distractions. No one else should be riding in the immediate area.

- Suitable horse or pony that is obedient, well trained to longe, and accustomed to being used for longe lessons. His gaits must be regular, steady and comfortable, and he must respond to the instructor's commands. *Never try to teach a longe lesson on a green horse!*

- Instructor with knowledge and experience in longeing, able to longe the horse with complete control and safety, maintaining even gaits and making smooth transitions. The instructor must also have sufficient knowledge and teaching experience to teach the student at his level.

- Correctly fitted longeing equipment, including:

    Longe line and longe whip; boots or bandages for horse.

    Saddle that fits both horse and rider. The saddle may be fitted with a pommel strap (safety strap), which the rider may hold to secure his position, or a neck strap may be used.

    Snaffle bridle.

    A longe cavesson, fitted correctly over the bridle (noseband fastened inside bridle cheekpieces), is the best choice of headgear.

    Side reins may be used to help maintain a steady balance and frame, but only on well-schooled, experienced horses and *only* by instructors who can fit them correctly and understand their proper use. (Longeing with side reins is an advanced skill and is not appropriate for most Pony Club longe lessons. Incorrect use of side reins can damage the horse's training and can be dangerous.)

    Both instructor and rider should wear safe and suitable attire, including a correctly fitted ASTM/SEI safety helmet, with chin strap fastened, and appropriate footwear.

Giving a longe lesson.

1. Instructor and student safely dressed for longeing and riding.
2. Horse wears longe cavesson, boots/bandages, properly fitted side reins.
3. Bridle reins secured; student holds neckstrap, pommel, or safety strap.
4. Longe in safe, enclosed area with good footing.

PROCEDURE FOR GIVING A LONGE LESSON

Longe the horse first without the rider, in both directions, until he is settled and obedient.

If side reins are used, they must *always* be unfastened before the rider mounts or dismounts. This is a safety measure which allows the horse freedom of his head and neck and prevents the rider from getting caught in the side reins while mounting or dismounting. Never leave the side reins fastened to the saddle in a loop which could catch the rider's leg.

When the horse is ready, halt and let the rider mount and adjust the stirrups. A student new to longe lessons should be longed at a walk (with reins and stirrups) until he or she is relaxed, confident, and accustomed to the size of the longeing circle.

At first, let the rider get used to the longeing circle and begin to feel the movement of the horse. Encourage the rider to breathe deeply, to sit deep and tall, to look up and forward, and to become aware of the way the horse moves under him. Be careful to longe the horse steadily and quietly, to make smooth transitions, and to prepare both horse and rider for any transition or new exercise. Abrupt transitions can affect the rider's balance and confidence.

Next, the rider will learn how to ride without reins. Show your student how to rest his hands lightly on the pommel and how to hold the pommel or safety strap if he begins to lose his balance or feel insecure. *Emphasize that he must never grab the reins to save his balance.* At this point, the bridle reins can be secured over the horse's neck and are no longer needed. However, they should always be within reach in case of emergency.

Have the rider perform simple exercises to help him or her get used to riding without reins, such as:

- Large arm circles, one arm at a time.

- Reaching forward to stroke the horse on the neck, then reaching back to stroke him behind the saddle.

- Arm circles and shoulder circles, first with alternating arms and then with both arms at once.

- Stretching both arms up over the head; touching knees; touching toes.

- Extending both arms straight out from the shoulders and alternately twisting the trunk to the left and right.

- Riding with arms extended out from the shoulders, hands on head, arms folded, and with hands in riding position as if holding reins.

In all exercises, emphasize that the object is to stay balanced and supple, and to develop a secure, independent seat. This means that the seat, legs, and lower body stay in a good position even when the arms and upper body are performing exercises (or vice versa). (For further descriptions of exercises, see *The United States Pony Club Manual of Horsemanship: Basics for Beginners/D Level*, pages 50–55 and 89–97.)

Arm circles and shoulder exercises.

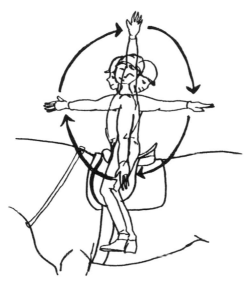

1. Arm circles

2. Shoulder circles

Stretching exercises

1. Stretching arms up
2. Touching toes

3. Touching opposite toe

Let the rider develop confidence at posting trot and sitting trot with stirrups, holding the pommel or safety strap if necessary. Keep the trot slow, steady, and quiet. Encourage the rider to gradually let go of the pommel or safety strap, first with one hand, and finally, when he is confident, with both hands. Emphasize that he should take hold of the pommel or safety strap to save his balance or to correct his position, but release his hold on it when he feels secure.

The next stage depends on the rider's level and needs and the instructor's judgment. Some students will need further work with stirrups in order to develop confidence, balance, and security. Others will be ready to go on to work without stirrups.

Depending on the rider's level and fitness, the rest of the longe lesson may consist of more exercises, position work, transitions, and variations of pace. Remember to work equally on both sides for the benefit of both horse and rider. Give frequent, short rest breaks to avoid overstressing the rider's muscles and concentration. Longeing is hard work; 10 minutes may be plenty for a novice, and 20 minutes is quite demanding even for a fit, experienced rider and horse.

When your student is ready to work without stirrups, cross the stirrup irons over in front of the pommel (pull the leathers out 6 to 8 inches from the stirrup bar, and fold them so that they lie flat). Work at the walk until the rider is confident and comfortable in the correct position. Practicing leg exercises (leg stretches, ankle circles, and so on) and repeating some easy loosening exercises help develop confidence and a secure seat. Remind your student to secure his seat and reposition himself when necessary by holding the pommel or safety strap instead of tensing up and gripping with his legs.

Crossing stirrups.

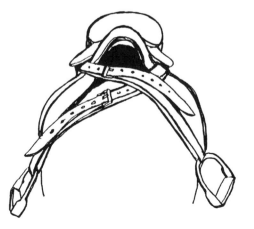

Pull buckles out 6 inches or so, and make sure both straps lie flat under the skirt of the saddle.

Leg exercises.

1. Point toes up and down.

2. Ankle circles

3. Leg swings

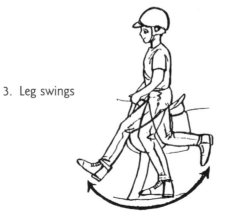

The following exercises will help the rider develop good balance and position without stirrups:

- At halt or walk, stretch both legs slowly downward, slightly backward, and out to the side from the hip joint. Hold for a few seconds, then release and let the legs return to the horse's side. This helps lower the knees, flatten the thighs, and improve the rider's leg position. Be careful not to arch the back, tip forward, or exaggerate the stretch.

- Bring knees and thighs off the saddle (sideways), then allow them to fall back into position. Don't take them too far off or hold for too long, or cramping may result. This emphasizes balance on the seat bones and allows the legs to hang correctly under the body.

- Ride sitting trot, posting trot, and half-seat without stirrups (but keep the duration and level of work within the student's capabilities).

- Upper-body exercises, such as arm circles, side swings, and arms out to the side, performed without stirrups first at a walk, later at a sitting trot.

Exercises for balance without stirrups.

 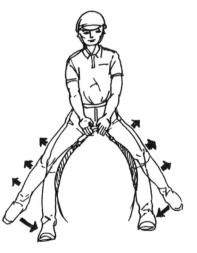

1. Stretch both legs back and down from the hip joint. (Don't tip forward, overarch the back, or overdo this stretch.)

2. Bring knees and thighs off saddle (sideways); allow them to fall back into position.

Riding without reins or stirrups on the longe.

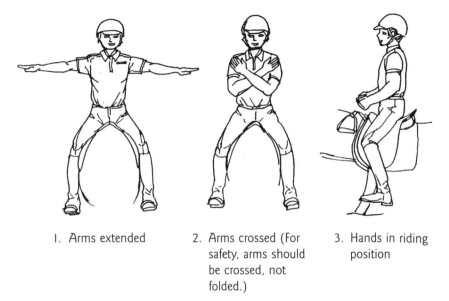

1. Arms extended

2. Arms crossed (For safety, arms should be crossed, not folded.)

3. Hands in riding position

Only advanced riders on experienced longe horses should be allowed to canter on the longe. These riders may practice canter transitions and exercises at the canter for short periods.

For advanced riders, it is useful to practice transitions and work in all gaits with the hands in a riding position, as if holding reins. Always be aware of position, balance, and suppleness. Only a rider whose position is basically correct and supple will be able to stay in balance. If a rider becomes insecure or loses his balance and position for any reason, the horse should be brought back to a walk while the rider corrects his own position. Even fit, experienced riders should take frequent short rest breaks, which can be used for discussion.